Our NHS
for better or worse?

Dr Ruth Chambers OBE

Copyright

© Dr Ruth Chambers OBE asserts her rights under the Copyright, Designs and Patents Act 1988 to be identified as the author of this work.
All rights reserved. No part of this publication may be reproduced, stored in a retrieval system or transmitted, in any form or by any means, electronic, mechanical, photocopying, recording or otherwise, without the prior permission of the copyright owner.

Cartoons by John Byrne.

ISBN 9798341298170

Date of publication - October 2024

Disclaimer

The content of this book is based on Dr Ruth's take on the ups and downs of her medical career, and her perspectives of the national advice and guidance relating to the National Health Service across the UK. Inclusion of named agencies, websites, companies or services in this book does not constitute a recommendation or an endorsement. The stories and insights about their experiences of the NHS that Dr Ruth has gleaned from the very many people that she has chatted to, have been combined and collated and mainly anonymized, to relay the perspectives of NHS staff and patients. All proceeds from sales of this book will be donated to the Douglas Macmillan Hospice in North Staffordshire.

Dr Ruth Chambers FRCGP, MD, OBE

Dr Ruth was a general practitioner for 40+ years. She is a Visiting Professor at Staffordshire University and also Honorary Professor at Keele University. Ruth's interests focus on aiding people to self-care, evolving effective ways of working and many other health related themes - most recently the adoption of technology enabled care services in the NHS. She is a co-director of Raparu Consult CIC. Ruth has worked with the Royal College of General Practitioners, Department of Health/NHS England, the Human Fertilisation Authority and other healthcare organisations on various projects over the last three decades. Fifteen years ago, Ruth led on establishing a Quality Improvement Framework across Stoke-on-Trent general practices which has raised standards at scale on a wide range of measures - improved clinical practice and patients' health outcomes (her reward was getting an OBE!). Ruth has written 83 other books, mainly for health professionals, but eight have been for the general public on stress, heart disease, back pain and how technology can empower people to self-care; four of her books have been translated into other languages - Japanese, Italian and Korean. If you want to know more about her medical career - read up on Dr Ruth's achievements in Who's Who, or take a look at her website www.ruthchambers.co.uk

Acknowledgements

I should like to thank Chris, my husband, for the support he's given me in creating this book – and of course, in helping with our family life whilst I developed my career paths and zipped around doing all sorts of research and educational projects, combined with being a busy GP.

My thanks to all those NHS staff and members of the public whom I've talked to in evolving this book, for your insights into the NHS and relaying your experiences of delivering or receiving healthcare – over the last 50 years and nowadays. I've included all your insights and experiences in reasonably anonymized ways, sometimes by combining or linking your personal stories. My grateful thanks too to Paula and Fr John Stather who've helped me to stay motivated in completing this book, and have formatted and edited the content for publication.

Contents

Foreword		1
Chapter 1	How the NHS operated in 1970s… and does Now!	2
Chapter 2	See, Do, Share – Dr Ruth's routes to fame	46
Chapter 3	Gender issues – across our NHS	64
Chapter 4	How stressful is working in the NHS?	79
Chapter 5	Asylum, or so called sanctuary	89
Chapter 6	Whistleblowing, or not?	100
Chapter 7	Dispensing with(in) the rules!	114
Chapter 8	Obesity – a huge problem!	131
Chapter 9	Prison healthcare	144
Chapter 10	End of life?	157
Chapter 11	Digital transformation of healthcare - very trying!	170
Chapter 12	Prescription for Change: 77 ways to save and sustain the NHS	199
Abbreviations		209

Foreword

I've loved being a doctor for the last 50 years; and I think that my patients have appreciated my care for them and their loved ones too! I've been motivated to progress along a very bumpy career path across the NHS as a GP and with academic roles, when apart from some excellent practice, I've spotted wrong doing, or sub-standard quality of care - and taken actions. That's usually worked out well so that I've actively contributed to many local and national programmes to improve the delivery of NHS care over the years, captured here in the various chapters.

The focus is on the THEN and NOW relating to our NHS workforce and how hospital and general practice and community healthcare exist together, gender discrimination of staff, the unfair treatment of people in mental asylums and inadequate health care in prisons, the burdening pressure on the NHS from people's unhealthy lifestyle habits such as obesity, how we need to listen to whistleblowers and be vigilant for any signs of fraud. The NOW capture is nearly always positive for each of these chapters and praises the achievements we've made for end-of-life care, and the evolving digital operation and delivery of care at increasing scale in the NHS.

But this book isn't just about me and my experiences. I've talked to very many others working in the NHS and social care, or who have been service users. They provide the reader with a wide range of truthful 'stories' and insights relaying the changes (for good or bad) in the delivery of NHS care and inter-related public services – with a special focus on general practice which is central to the NHS, and critical to its survival. Clinicians' and NHS staff's passion to care shines out throughout the book.

The final chapter of the book draws on all these insider stories and my vast experience to conclude what must happen now at scale, to build on the best parts of the NHS and repair the gaps (funding, delivery, workforce, culture, preventive care) despite the difficulties. This is the prescription for change that we need – 77 brilliant ideas to save and sustain our NHS.

Chapter 1. How the NHS operated in 1970s... and does Now!

Let's get the NHS in context

When the NHS was established in 1948, it was a service focused on episodes of care, which was accessed by patients either visiting their GP or going to hospital to see a doctor as an outpatient, or to be admitted. The founding principles of the NHS were that services should be comprehensive, universal and free at the point of delivery, based on a person's clinical need and not their ability to pay for treatment, apart from some dental and optical care. Providing free healthcare was a main pledge of the Labour government's manifesto in 1945. The then Minister of Health, Aneurin Nye Bevan, led on the plan and the legislation came into force for the establishment of the NHS in 1948, despite a range of opposition. It was not to be regarded as a 'charity', but funded by tax payers.

Changes in population demographics such as people living longer, patterns of disease, the range of available treatments and technologies have inevitably created the need to establish a more joined up, co-ordinated and collaborative health and care system. For decades, GPs were seen as the 'gatekeepers' of the NHS, for all the patients registered with their practices, providing continuity of healthcare for 24 hours a day, seven days a week. It was the GP who was first on the scene when a patient called for help and would then decide if they could sort the problem themselves, or call an ambulance to arrange a hospital admission or send the patient into A&E. GPs worked without any specific contractual agreement that defined their clinical responsibilities for many decades, and their clinical care was very much based on trust. This changed drastically with government-led changes in 2004, though the expectation was retained for general practice teams to provide continuing care from the start to the end of patient pathways.

In the 1960s

I got talking to Ann in a coffee shop recently who had worked at our local Royal Infirmary (as hospitals were termed in those days) as a medical secretary, from 1959 when she was aged 16 years old.

She got married four years later and stopped work soon afterwards, as it was then the norm for married women to be home based. She started without any training or security checks and with full access to all the patients' medical records, typing up hospital consultants' notes and letters in the different ways that they expected. For instance, an orthopaedic consultant just dictated their notes using abbreviations like 'AJ' to describe the type of operation they'd performed, whereas medical physicians and paediatricians gave her their scribbled written notes to type up, so she quickly learnt to read doctors' handwriting. She had a medical dictionary on her desk so that she could get the medical terminology spelling right. Ann said that in those days, hospital consultants 'were seen as gods'! They were all male doctors as far as she can remember, and she's not aware that there were any male nurses at all then.

In the 1970s

My first job as a fully practising doctor was in my fifth year at university in 1974 when it was acceptable for a medical student to be employed by the hospital as a locum doctor, to cover for the junior doctor who was away on holiday. That enabled me to get a taste of what my working life was really going to be like, and I was able to take on all of the doctor's powers - prescribing drugs, certifying deaths, checking out and treating patients' various health problems, initiating cardiac resuscitation - without being registered as a doctor with the General Medical Council. These days a junior doctor even when they are qualified would need to be supervised in prescribing medication during their first year working as a medic. I have proof that I was definitely employed by the hospital more than 50 years ago, as my NHS pension was calculated in a small part on the amount that I was paid for that two weeks locum, in that year. In those days doctors signed the Hippocratic Oath when they qualified, and one of the promises in that is to 'do no harm'; hopefully I and my fellow students managed to attain that goal as unqualified and minimally supervised student locum doctors!

When I worked as a junior doctor in 1976 in my second post at what is now called Royal Stoke University Hospital, it consisted of two completely separate hospitals that operated independently, despite being based 500 yards or so apart. Each hospital had an accident and emergency department and parallel medical specialties, except for paediatrics where the clinical teams delivered their care across both hospitals. Patients just turned up at A&E where they were always seen and triaged by a nurse who handled the patient or referred them to a doctor of mid-grade, who referred them to a consultant if need be. People were never sent away to return later or kept waiting for hours, as they often are today. Now the Royal Stoke University Hospital has merged with the County Hospital based in Stafford about 15 miles away to form the University Hospitals of North Midlands (UHNM) NHS Trust, which covers a population of around one million local people.

Another odd arrangement of inpatient care was that in the surgical wards where the patients who were overseen by my Consultant, Dr P, were placed, about one-quarter of the beds in a branch of the ward were reserved for his private patients. The NHS hospital had an arrangement with Dr P that he had the rights to use those beds and agreed timings in one of the theatres for performing surgery. He obviously did well out of the arrangement and in any ward round prioritised those private patients first. The thing was that as a junior doctor in his team, I had to cover the out of hours care of his private patients directly whenever I was on shift (about 90 hours as a typical working week in those days) and Dr P was at home – without me receiving any extra pay. And those patients who were paying for their care expected a rapid response and were somewhat demanding!

Hospital shifts were really tough in those days, for the junior doctors particularly. They were usually doing 'one in two' shifts, which meant working 34 hour shifts every other weekday, so starting at 8am on a Monday you slogged all day, evening and through the night and continued on the Tuesday until 6pm; then home for a break and welcome sleep, before starting at 8am on the Wednesday, working until 6pm on Thursday evening and back on Friday at 8am. If it was your hardest week you were then working over the weekend from 8am Saturday to Monday at 8am with the rest of Monday off to catch up on your sleep. At best you were doing about 90 hours a week and at worst if it was your alternate weekend on duty you were doing as many as 120 hours that week. You were paid the full hourly rate for 40 hours a week and only one-third of the hourly rate for all the extra hours you were contracted for. But if you left the ward late after a shift you wouldn't get a single penny more. In the 1980s, junior doctors were more likely to be on 'one in three' or 'one in four' rotas – still pretty hard work but better than being on site for twice as many nights and weekends as it was in the 1970s. During the overnight part of my 34 hours shift, I'd try and get some sleep on the floor of an office between midnight and 6am, but in that period I'd be waiting for emergency admissions to arrive from the A&E department, and then I'd get up, admit and triage the patient, and then organise their immediate clinical treatment. When I was doing obstetrics for six months during my GP training in the late 1970s, I really appreciated that the maternity ward had turned an office into a bedroom measuring 9 feet by 6 feet for the junior doctor who was on call to sleep in. It just had a bed and chair with no washing facilities, so I could usually bunk there in my work clothes for a good few hours as the maternity ward was usually quieter at night as many of the pregnant mums had been induced in the morning to trigger their labour, which usually resulted in their babies being born between noon and 6pm. If the midwives needed a doctor's help in the middle of the night, they'd bang on our bedroom door and drag us out to help to deliver the baby or stitch up a new mum.

One bonus of being a junior doctor in those days was getting free accommodation for each six months post for which you were contracted. You'd have your own bedroom in a nearby house or hospital building with a shared bathroom, kitchen and if you were lucky, lounge. You could access the doctors' mess to play snooker, (I got so good at snooker killing time on call as a junior doctor in my general surgery post that I even beat my father by the end of that six months placement), or help yourself to alcohol available in the bar and pay into an honesty box. The hospital restaurant would typically have a dedicated space reserved for the doctors and the rest of the floor was for other hospital staff or visitors. Alcohol flowed freely, even if one of the doctors was 'on call' for one or more of the hospital wards. I didn't drink much alcohol – but that meant I had to provide cover for the junior doctors who did, as it was thought okay in those days to be drinking alcohol on duty. It was common for staff, visitors and patients to smoke in the hospital corridors and even the wards then too. Again, I didn't – but I did eat the chocolates and cakes that many grateful patients gave us when they were discharged (so I wasn't perfect!).

Nurses were housed, free, in the hospital grounds very close to the wards too. My friend Tim recalls how his then girlfriend Maggie lived in the nursing block when she'd qualified to work as a nurse, but men were not allowed in after 10pm. But on the other hand, like other boyfriends he learnt to sneak in when it was quiet but had to leave via the fire exit as the entry door was guarded by a senior ward sister from 10pm onwards. But doctors and their visitors could come and go to, and from, their hospital based accommodation at any time of the day or night, as they were often on call and trusted to behave properly.

There was a real team bond amongst the ward doctors who were known as the 'firm', in those days. In my first junior doctor role, the hospital consultant insisted that we all play golf with him on a Wednesday afternoon, about 10 miles away from the hospital, as six or so members of the firm. The team of doctors on the neighbouring ward covered for us whilst we were away. Most of us had not played golf before and really did not want to allocate our few spare hours to doing so, but we had no choice. This hospital 'god' expected us to do his bidding! For my next few years of working in hospital whatever firm I was part of would have supper together about once a month- at someone's house or even at a local pub. On Christmas day, the head doctor of the firm would come into the ward at lunchtime and carved the turkey even if they weren't on duty – for the patients and the staff. Even if you were off duty as a junior doctor that Christmas day, you were still expected to come in – as the firm was your family now.

If I was unsure about how to manage a patient when I was on night duty, working on my own as a junior doctor, I would go to the registrar if they were available, a mid-grade doctor halfway up the career ladder to being a consultant. But if they were unavailable e.g. operating in theatre I'd just ring the consultant who'd be at home or out with friends and describe the problem, and then they'd usually advise me what medical action to take. They generally instructed us from afar by phone, rather than come personally into the hospital to help with the acutely unwell patients out of hours – delegation, delegation, delegation!!

That family ethos in the NHS workforce applied to everyone who was employed there. Graham was telling me that he worked in estates at the same Royal Stoke hospital that I did in the 1970s and 1980s. He was put on the waiting list for a knee operation for which it was usually at least a 20 weeks wait (a very long time in those days!) when the consultant looked at his records and realised that he worked at the hospital. "Oh, you're one of us" he said and logged Graham in as a priority for an operation later that week. In those days, 'they looked after their own'!

Ann started working for the NHS as a nursing cadet aged 16 years old, at first as an auxiliary worker for three days a week, alongside studying for her A levels for two days a week. Even with no experience or formal training she handled prescription drugs in the mental hospital she worked in and she remembers how nearly every patient was given a red, round tablet (imipramine) for their depression, anxiety and even bed wetting. There were no prior personal security checks of staff in those days and Ann could have helped herself to as many of those tablets as she liked, giving her patients a few smarties instead – no-one would have noticed as so much of anyone's work was done on trust, and usually without any supervision!

When Julie became a student nurse in 1972, she was interviewed for the role by the hospital matron. The matron wore a frilly hat and bow under her chin to indicate her seniority. Julie signed up to a three years academic course that involved working unpaid on the hospital wards for most of the time, learning as a frontline, hands-on student nurse with a small proportion of teaching being done in classrooms. Another part of the student nurse's code was not to get pregnant – or married whilst undertaking their training; if you did you were out and off the course. Once she became a state registered nurse three years later, she wore a full cap with cuffs at the end of her sleeves, to relay that she was qualified and no longer a student nurse. She was not allowed to wear her nurse's uniform outside the hospital, and so arrived at the hospital in her own clothes to get changed there, ready for work. "It was all part of the discipline" she said.

When Pat trained to be a nurse in the 1970s, a newly qualified nurse just had to pay £1.50 as a one-off to the General Nursing Council to become a state registered nurse. There were no university or college fees then whereas these days a student can typically qualify with at least £40,000 debt for fees and living expenses for the three years nursing course. Pat moved on from being a ward nurse in elderly care after she qualified to becoming a 'health visitor' in the community. But as with so many other clinical roles, the numbers of health visitors employed in the NHS now has plummeted in the last few years.

In those days, once you became a registered nurse you got no extra training and just worked on the hospital wards to which you were allocated, dealing with whoever was admitted and whatever was in front of you. At 7am there was a shift change as the night staff went home, and for the nurses starting their day shift the routine was to make the beds and wash and feed the patients. The cleaners arrived at 9am and were seen as very friendly 'ward maids'. The doctors' ward rounds would start at 9am and all the staff (junior doctors and nurses) would group around the consultant and move on from patient to patient, listing the jobs to do once the ward round was finished. Timing was strict – the ward round would finish around 11am, lunch was dished out at 1pm for the 40 or so patients in each ward, and visitors could see their loved ones only between 2.30-4pm. I was talking to Jim the other day about his memory of having a hernia repair when he was aged 4 years old in 1973. He'd said good bye to his parents at the door into the paediatric ward as it was outside visiting hours and then had to change into hospital clothes in the toilet, as he wasn't allowed on the ward in his own garments. He was put in a cot with bars on, which felt like a cell as there was no bed available. Jim had his fifth birthday whilst an inpatient; his parents brought him in a birthday cake but the nurses ate it all, so he didn't even get a bite of it!

Becoming a GP in the 1970s didn't require any extra training after the initial 12 months as a junior doctor working in two consecutive six months hospital jobs. I got a little taste of what it was like running a full-on general practice service in 1977. I did a two weeks locum for a solo GP who practised in the countryside in Derbyshire. At that time I was just 25 years old and part-way through my second year of hospital training as a junior doctor, when I saw the advert for the two weeks locum. I thought that I would give it a go, allocating two of the four weeks of my precious annual leave that June, to test out whether I really did want to be a GP, as my future career. With no experience of general practice at all I just moved into Dr Barbara's house one Friday evening. She showed me my bedroom and we walked into the consultation room, opened the cupboards where the drugs were stored and I looked in the fridge for any medications that needed to be kept cool. Dr Barbara pointed out the stethoscope that I could use and other equipment, then passed me her doctor's bag full of drugs and medical equipment. She explained how Janet would be there in the practice as the only receptionist for three hours each weekday from Monday, but otherwise I'd be the one answering the one and only practice phone, booking patients in to be seen (though they mainly came and queued outside the door from 7.30am each weekday) and responding to any urgent call outs relayed at any time of the day or night on that same phone. There were no nurses or other clinical staff connected with the practice. Then with that 30 minutes introductory update she drove off on her holiday, only to be seen again 16 days later, when I had finished my sixteen x 24 hours shifts as THE locum GP for the 1,500 or so patients registered with Dr Barbara in that rural village. Luckily, the pharmacy assistant job I'd done in my school holidays as a teenager helped me to understand how to dispense the medicines that I prescribed for my new patients; and write prescriptions retrospectively for any emergency medicines that I pulled out of the doctor's bag for patients whom I saw at the practice or in their own homes, who were acutely unwell. There was a lot I didn't know though – like prescribing contraceptive pills. That topic had never cropped up in my medical student training nor the hospital based 20 months of jobs I'd done as a novice doctor. Nor had I ever taken the contraceptive pill myself. I had to blag it, pretending I was a more experienced doctor than I was and making excuses to look things up in medical handbooks or the drug formulary in the midst of a patient consultation. When she returned, Dr Barbara got good feedback about me as her locum from patients and the part-time receptionist, so she did ask me to help her out again a few months later, but by that time I was about to start my three years formal GP training in Bristol. In those days, being a GP was not regarded as a specialism. I wanted to be the best GP that I could be so I was in the minority of doctors in those days who opted for supported training in a mix of hospital and community settings to gain a much wider postgraduate experience across many hospital specialties like obstetrics, psychiatry, infectious diseases – that would better prepare me for the wide scope of a GP career. I did have my first child in the middle of that training programme, and I had to mask my extreme pregnancy sickness. It was so unusual to have a female doctor in a hospital post that it was seen as a 'let down' for me to be pregnant. I even vomited at work over a patient I was examining - luckily as this was a female patient she was forgiving and understood.

I had the right problem solving skills for becoming a GP, and I was prepared to act on my instincts about the best options for a patient. It seems a bit extreme looking back, but I even took a 70 year old patient, Ona, back to my home one day whom I met by chance in a hospital outpatient clinic having recently returned to work after my maternity leave. She was sitting in a corner of the waiting room in floods of tears and I went over and sat beside her and asked her what was wrong. Ona said she was frightened that terrorists were out to get her mistaking the flat that she lived in for her neighbour's; someone had left a note under her door the night before threatening that they would break into her own flat and injure her. She said she'd nowhere else to go as her family were away on holiday, so I believed her and took her to stay at my home. Ona stayed with me, my husband and our four months old baby son for a few weeks until her family returned and she was back to normal. I took her to the local police to report the threats and handover the note the next day – they didn't believe her (I'm not sure if I do retrospectively – but as a doctor you tend to give a patient the benefit of the doubt, until circumstances prove otherwise).

I've got better examples of helping people out of the blue but possibly then putting my family at risk. Walking along the path in a town centre pushing my baby Dave in his pram, I spotted a man who seemed to have collapsed in his car over his steering wheel. I shouted for help and a man nearby helped me to pull the man out of the car and lie him down on the pavement. I could not find a pulse and he was unconscious so I screeched for someone to phone 999 and I got on with doing cardio-resuscitation, thumping his chest and breathing directly with my mouth to his mouth, as I'd no equipment with me. It worked, and by the time the ambulance arrived eight or so minutes later he was breathing and alive, though still confused, and by then there were about ten passers-by looking on, clustered around us. That's when I realised that I'd lost sight of my son Dave – but he was still in his pushchair being looked after by a nice young lady. So, all went well – although I realised afterwards that I'd prioritised the patient's life over the safety and wellbeing of my own little boy.

I've always been aware of the sacrifices (and gains) that doctors who've qualified abroad have made in coming to work in the UK – in hospitals and general practices. I've got to know many international medical graduate (IMG) doctors, as they're called, pretty well over the years – who've mainly come from India, Pakistan, African countries like Nigeria and now South Africa, and more recently refugee doctors from Afghanistan, Sudan and Iran. One doctor from India wrote recently about how he'd set up his own general practice from scratch in the late 1970s in Bury, a fairly deprived area of England. He's still practising and now has a 9,000 patient population. When he first came to England he expected to return to work in India – but he didn't. He came to the UK as a qualified paediatrician, but soon switched to working in general practice as he liked being more in charge, and has developed a business side in his medical practice as he now owns two nursing homes nearby too.

Thinking back, the best bit about going to work as a doctor in the 1970s, whether in a hospital or a GP setting was being part of a team of people who consistently worked together as clinicians and support staff, dedicated to patient care, but having some fun along the way. Like it being the norm at the end of a substantive placement for the junior doctor or nurse to be thrown in a bath of water on the hospital ward with their clothes on by the team, unless you realised that 'fun' was coming and ran off (to preserve your bleep from getting wet of course!).

Real team work is what we had in place then as a norm. It's the team that make the less good bits of the day bearable, like dealing with rude behaviour from patients or them making unreasonable demands and complaints, outside your control.

In the 1980s
It was still common practice in the early 1980s for hospital managers to use doctors for whatever purpose they could, rather than be too concerned as to whether they were properly trained for taking on the responsibilities. When I went for a part-time job soon after I had had my second child, I worked as a doctor for a day care unit at Stockport

hospital Monday – Friday mornings. I was so good and quick at seeing the patients there that the hospital wanted to make more of my sessions and without any extra hours/pay or updated contract, I also became the doctor overseeing two geriatric intermediate care wards with about 50 patients between them, as I recall. I had no specialist training – I just did what was required. That was a one hour ward round with the ward manager, reviewing the patients whom the nurses had highlighted, and sorting them out medically, however complex their conditions. One of the bonuses of this job was getting 'crem' fees, for completing the first of two cremation forms needing to be signed off by two separate doctors. All of the patients on my wards were near death, so it was usual for two or three of them to die each week, and as I was the last responsible doctor to see them, I'd need to complete their 'crem' form, for which I'd receive payment from the undertaker. The 'ash cash' as it was called then would have been around £30 in the 1980s, so having nearly £100 some weeks was a lot of money to receive, extra to my sessional pay. It was a real treat because when I had worked at the Nottingham hospital in my first junior doctor job, the hospital management kept the 'ash cash' without any individual doctor's permission, to fund the sports centre for staff that was being built in the hospital grounds; I didn't even benefit from playing squash there as it was not open for use until after I'd moved on from my junior doctor job there in 1975.

In those days confidentiality was not a priority. Kevin who was a nurse on a urology ward remembers how strict the ward sister was about everyone (patients and nursing staff) needing to be silent when she was reviewing all the patients, so that she wasn't distracted from her lists of tasks. She would shout across the ward to different patients all about their medical complaints (this was a routine way of doing ward rounds, with no patient confidentiality). He remembers that one man who had erectile dysfunction, had had an implant fitted; the sister shouted across the ward to advise him how to sustain an erection of his penis. The whole ward of patients and staff were listening and chuckling!!

I was very lucky to be successful in getting to be a partner in a GP practice in the village of Stone in Staffordshire, in 1985. It was the norm then for as many as 100 doctors to compete to join a GP partnership and very unusual for a woman doctor to be successful. My experience of being employed as a salaried GP in a rural village for three years with little control over my job role had included being the main GP in a local asylum (see Chapter 5) and witnessing prescription fraud (see Chapter 7). I wanted to be more in control of my medical role as a GP partner. That sessional GP role had also included a three-week stretch twice a year, where I worked/ was on-call for 504 hours without a break, when my GP employer was on lengthy family holidays abroad and I was completely responsible night and day for the 2,300 or so registered patients. I had an initial interview at the practice with the doctors which was pretty casual, and more like checking me out. My real interview was with the four GP partners and their wives and my husband too, at a pretty formal dinner at Dr Will's house. We passed! I was the first woman GP within about a 10 miles radius at that time. Our contract was very strict and here's a few bits I've pulled out of an old document that I've found:

'The capital of the partnership shall ……..comprise the medicines, instruments, implements, reference books, records, furnishings and other assets of the present practice at the partnership premises and the money standing at the partnership bank account. Each partner will own a share in the capital proportionate to his share in the profits of the partnership……..:

	Dr. W	Dr. K	Dr. T	Dr. C	Dr. C (Ruth)
From 1985	22%	22%	22%	22%	12%

The profits and losses of the partnership shall belong to, and be borne by, the partners….'

It was only after I had accepted the post and started work that I realised I was to get a lesser share of the partnership profits (12% instead of a fairer 20%) for the first three years. When those three years expired, I would get a full share. I went with it and colluded in the same arrangement for an incoming partner three years later. There were other strict rules too stated as: 'If a partner becomes pregnant she has the right to: take reasonable time off from the practice for ante-natal care; and absent herself from the practice for a period of maternity leave commencing normally not before 11 weeks prior to the expected week of confinement and continuing for not longer than 29 weeks following the birth.' But!! 'In the event of the partner failing to return to full activity by 29 weeks following the birth of the baby (unless incapacitated) the remaining partners will be entitled to give due notice to the partner that she must retire from the practice.'

Being a GP in the 1980s was very hard work. The family doctor would be the first person that a patient would call if they or a loved one, were really unwell. So, GPs did very much what paramedics do now as first attenders. If it was during the day, the receptionist would take the call and might book the person in the GPs' surgery to be seen by a doctor or nurse that same day, or put the call through to the doctor, interrupting their current patient consultation, to decide if they were going to see the patient in person at their home as an emergency straight away, or later in the day after their surgery had finished.

Dr Ken describes the family doctor surgery where he worked as being like a second family, a home from home. This became his professional home for 40 years. In the 1980s and for a couple of decades afterwards GPs regarded hospital specialists and their secretaries as kindred professionals too. This included the teams of district, health visitor and psychiatric nurses, probation and social workers, and local pharmacists. Their exchanges were mostly personal, chatty and direct, helping each other shoulder the burdens of providing person-centred continuity of care.

In those days, nurses did delegated tasks from the doctor, for example catheterising a patient if the patient was unable to pee. Auxiliary nurses working in hospitals could catheterise; female auxiliary nurses could catheterise men and women, but male auxiliary nurses were only permitted to catheterise men.

Home visits were very common in the 1970s - 2010. I'd sit with my GP partners signing off prescriptions after our morning surgeries, drinking coffee or tea and we'd divide up the requested home visits fairly, trying to balance a particular patient who usually saw 'Dr X' with the geographical spread of the requested visits. These were the acute visits requested that day for individual patients in their own homes or in care or nursing homes, done between morning and afternoon surgeries, as well as the out of hours ones who were seen later on, alongside those patients whom the GP judged needed to be followed-up, such as being at the end of their lives. Home visits really built your relationships with the patients and their families – well usually anyway if there was a good outcome for whoever was ill. Patients were very grateful for their home visits and would often offer the visiting doctor a cup of tea, or even a sherry or glass of wine, especially if it was a special time like Christmas Day or Boxing Day or a bank holiday.

Dave who's had a nursing career that's gone from hands on nursing care in the 1980s to chairing an NHS senior board in 2024 shares that "All the way through my nursing career, what I've seen predominately from the staff is kindness." He's always been a doer: in the 1980s, he reorganised ward rounds so instead of waiting for a consultant to come and bark the orders, Dave re-organised the ward team to be primed and ready so that the ward round ran more efficiently, extending the attending team members to include a physiotherapist, an occupational therapist and pharmacist, as well as junior doctors and nurses. He had the medical notes out ready for the consultant, having done initial triaging of each patient ready for the consultant. The first time he trialled this the consultant was taken aback by the unexpected team approach, but allowed the trial to go ahead and said at the end of the round: "I've learnt so much about how we can do ward rounds in future!". The team were impressed and relieved, as they had expected the consultant to be arrogant and refuse to cooperate.

As a family doctor I was expected to be part of the local community, and my eldest son still remembers as a child being dragged along to the local fete in town, as his GP mum was expected to attend such events and bring the family along. As the years went by my kids refused to go in the local supermarket with me, as individual shoppers would often block me in the aisle to ask intimate medical questions about their health matters, like test results or discuss new symptoms that they were experiencing.

In the 1990s

In the 1990s there was still huge competition to get a GP post. Just like me ten years earlier Dr Paul was interviewed by the prospective GP partners, with his wife. Most wives didn't work in those days, but his did, as a lawyer. When he started in the practice where he successfully applied to be a GP partner he covered his share of the on call duties. So that was dealing with all the emergency calls between 6pm – 8am, as well as his usual daytime consultation sessions, working each day either side of that night shift without a break, once a week and every fifth weekend (with extra shifts if a partner was away or ill). He and his four GP partners (one of whom was a woman- still unusual then) and two nurses worked with 6.5 minutes appointments per patient, which included writing up the notes on the patient's paper record. But patient reviews were less complex in those days as so many health conditions that are prioritised now wouldn't have been recognised then, and hospital care included looking after patients, say, with diabetes, which has been delegated to GPs to oversee these days. Because he was married his wife could help by taking calls when he was called out visiting a patient at night; but previously when Dr Paul was covering out of hours for a different practice in his final year as a GP trainee, he had had to stay with one of the receptionists at their home overnight, as she took any night time phone calls from patients if, and when, he was out doing home visits for others.

Dr Paul was one of the local GP leaders who helped to set up the GP Cooperative, the local 'deputising service' in Northern Staffordshire called the 'Coop' in the mid-1990s, to cover out of hours work provided by local GPs across 30 or so practices, with an overall patient population of around 200,000. Other areas set up their own too, but some practices declined to join in, as they still wanted to provide 24 hours care personally to their own patients, in their way. The Coop had a good team culture and trained triage nurses to handle the initial telephone calls; just as receptionists would do in the practice during the day, but applying their clinical knowledge too. They did not use algorithms then as the 111 service does today giving more or less automated responses to those ringing in; they conducted person-centred patient reviews before selecting the care pathway or advice to fit the patient's needs and preferences.

The camaraderie of being one of the practice GP team kept Dr Sharon going in the 1990s. She could ask any other GP for help with a particular patient, as could the practice nurses. She liked working in a deprived area as she could make a real difference to her patients, who often presented late on with their health problems. She remembers a patient in her late 40s who came to see her after being discharged from hospital with tummy pain as the staff there thought she would be okay. Dr Sharon's instinct was that this was an alarming problem, so she organised an urgent abdominal scan for the patient that confirmed a serious tumour, that was rapidly operated on in hospital. A few weeks later the patient and her friend came back to see Dr Sharon to thank her personally for listening to her and acting so fast.

Follow-on care by the same GP was still the norm in the 1990s, just as it had been for decades before. June remembers her GP who lived and practised nearby popping into her neighbour's house every weekday morning whilst her daughter who lived there too was out, to check that the older lady patient who was near death was doing okay in her daughter's absence! And for me, even though I was a very part-time GP, spending most of time doing academic work, I'd still step up as an emergency doctor if called upon. I was travelling abroad on holiday on a long-haul flight with my family, when a person collapsed on the aeroplane and a call went out from the flight staff for help from a doctor or nurse. I immediately left my family in their seats, got up in the midst of a lovely meal and assessed her. She survived and thanks to my intervention and the trusted help that I gave, the captain piloting the plane did not have to divert and stop in a nearby country on our way to our destination.

In the 1990s community mental health care was disentangled from that in established hospitals, which separated the provision of mental healthcare from acute secondary care. That gave mental health care more distinction as a separate entity, but the separation did mean that someone's physical and mental health was often treated in parallel by different teams, and not connected so well to be regarded as a 'whole person'.

When I was practising as a doctor in the 1990s, people automatically turned to their GPs when they were seriously ill - and the GPs came along when they called – rarely refusing to visit or directing them to phone for an ambulance instead. We were paid extra £s then by the local government system for doing an urgent home visit between 10pm and 7am. It wasn't a great deal, but was all part of how we were paid as general practice businesses, needing to generate a viable income and pay nursing staff and receptionists and cleaners, as well as paying for our premises and all the resources we needed like couches/equipment such as stethoscopes/ cleaning kits and syringes/ medication for emergencies or performing tasks like minor surgery. We were sometimes a bit naughty and if called out to a care home or a nursing home at night, might ask the staff if there was any other resident for whom they'd like a medical assessment. That often led to us seeing four different patients when called out to a home at midnight hours or 6am, which the home staff welcomed, and the extra funds made the emergency visit disrupting our sleep more worthwhile. And even if as a GP you'd done three or more emergency home visits to different places between 8pm and 8am say on one night, you still clocked in for work at your surgery on time the next day at 8.30am as usual. There was no catch up time to recover or make up for your disrupted sleep. And you had to be nice to your partner or house mate who'd been taking the emergency calls from your patients relayed to your home phoneline whilst you were out and about with your doctor's bag!

There were significant changes in the way that general practice operated then too with the NHS and Community Care Act that came into effect in 1990. The Act introduced the 'purchase/provider split' - separating the provision of care from the commissioning (that is, purchasing) of healthcare with a sort of internal market; the Trusts created took over the responsibility and management of hospitals and were more in charge of the finances. The new regulations also brought in payments based on achievement and higher expectations of delivery of care in general practice settings. Practices with more than 11,000 registered patients (later reduced to a minimum list size of 5,000) could become 'fundholders' if they wanted to take more control of their budget, and have more choice over where they purchased hospital and community services from, and more.

The increased working hours required to accommodate the paperwork from the national changes, led to more reported stress and exhaustion by GPs, most of whom were already working regular 24 hour days, regularly covering nights on call after tough 10 to 12 hour in-person care in their surgeries and doing home visits. My practice of five GP partners chummed up with a similarly sized practice in Stone; so, allowing for GPs to be taking holiday leave, we worked on average 10-12 hour days in the practice from 8am, with one half-day off during the week from around 2pm; and then we were on call for the two neighbouring practices of around 20,000 registered patients – covering every night and the entire weekend. So, I would take my turn to be on call during a weekday overnight with no break in that 35 hour 2-day shift (with busy evening visit requests from patients and my sleep likely to be interrupted once or twice doing home visits across a 10 mile stretch) and providing on-call on a Saturday or Sunday for 24 hours, about every four weeks, allowing for partners' holiday and sick leave.

In the 1990s it was usual for a local community hospital that employed health visitors, district nurses, mental health nurses, physiotherapists, chiropodists, phlebotomists to base them in a local general practice and pay marginal rental to the GP owners for the space. This enabled them to work closely with general practice teams, jointly looking after the same patients if their health condition warranted shared-care. But these community clinical teams moved out of many of their general practice bases around 2010. Nowadays such staff have lost that personal contact with general practice teams and often work in parallel paths, which disrupts the continuity of care that was previously the norm.

In the 2000s
Even in the early 2000s the team spirit and camaraderie still prevailed in hospital and general practice teams. Carol told me that on her ward on April Fools Day 2004, a senior paediatric nurse Dan put *Rescus Annie* in a cot, then hooked up a heart tracing device (ECG machine) to the 'doll' and pulled the curtains round. At hand over time as the nursing staff came on shift Dan alerted them that there was a critically ill baby in that bed space. As he left, he switched the ECG machine on so it started sounding the alarm as a joke, and left the ward. But what he didn't realise was that the nurses now on shift had been taken in by his ruse and so ran

to the bed space, whilst someone dialled for the crash team. When the intensive care team were made aware of the crash team being called they diverted a helicopter to them, that was already in flight to another hospital to pick up a critically ill child there! Disciplinary action ensued for nurse Dan.

Dr Alex described how even in the early 2000s doctors just muddled through. If a junior surgeon for example was insufficiently skilled to finish an operation, they'd shout for help from an experienced surgeon operating in a theatre next door and the expert doctor would just shout back detailed instructions to the junior doctor of what to do, and continue their operation, without going in person to the neighbouring theatre and viewing the patient.

Although junior doctors were no longer working 'one in two' days and nights on call as they were a few decades before, they were now expected to look after many more patients than junior doctors did 30 years previously. For example, Dr Sally remembers as a junior doctor at an Oxford hospital in 2005 looking after six medical wards in her first junior doctor post overnight – that was 160 patients!! Not very safe. And Dr Alex remembers after his overnight shift at the same hospital at that time, he often had to stay on until 11am or so (unpaid for three hours) to complete the remaining patient tasks after the early morning ward round. Then he'd go home very tired to get some sleep and come back for his next overnight shift later that day at 9pm.

Dr Carl remembers how hospital teams were getting more and more stretched at that time. One of the worst days he recalls was when he was a junior doctor working on the diabetes/endocrine ward. Norovirus was reported and as many patients as possible were discharged home that day with no new incoming patients. When he came back to work the next day, 24 new patients had been admitted after a deep clean of the ward. The other junior doctors were off sick and the consultant was in clinic. So, it was just junior Dr Carl on his own most of day with these 24 new patients; two died on the ward and two were admitted to intensive care. Dr Carl called for help and the hospital's chief executive came in and tried to call two consultants in, who arrived several hours later. Dr Carl was fire-fighting all day with no time to medically clerk any patients properly.

There was no subsequent investigation into whether patients had died as a result of the inadequate number of clinicians in the ward that day.

I know so many doctors who came from India to join our British medical workforce in the 2000s and since. Dr Jag came to the UK from India in 2002 when he did two, six months junior doctor jobs in a Blackburn hospital before starting GP specialty training for three years in the Lake District. He felt "very privileged to be working in the NHS, for the NHS". He had free accommodation in the hospitals and in Blackburn the housekeeper came in everyday to clean his room and change the bed sheets. He was given vouchers for using in the doctors' mess, so that he could get freely available food when he was working on call. Dr Jag has been working as a GP in the deprived area of Stoke-on-Trent ever since, and is one of the few full-time GPs whom I know nowadays who seems to be happy and dedicated in their current role.

In 2004, much changed with the national legislation for the new GP contract. This enabled GPs to relinquish 24 hours responsibility for providing patient care outside office hours (6pm – 8am) and so doctors' working lives were more doable. GPs often stayed on for an extra hour or so each evening finishing paperwork, but after 6pm they could pass the responsibility for providing cover to the local Out-of-Hours medical service providers, until 8am the next morning. That's unless the GP worked in a rural or very remote area – where providing out-of-hours cover could still be the responsibility of the local general practice unless they had passed their out of hours contract on e.g. to their local health board if based in Scotland. But this was the start for many patients of experiencing less continuity in the care they received from their GP, who was now only directly available for them, for ten hours a day.

Since 2010……

It seems like there's been constant reorganisation of the NHS over the last 20 years – that does not always make sense to the doctors, nurses and other NHS staff working on the ground, and distracts the senior managers from their primary purpose to improve and deliver consistently high quality healthcare. One feature is the emergence of Primary Care Networks (PCNs) in 2019; each usually has around four to six general practices, with a population size of 30,000 – 50,000, though some of the

1,250 or so PCNs in England are much larger. The government has recently donated extra funding per PCN for expanding the workforce employed in general practices via the Additional Roles Reimbursement Scheme (ARRS) to improve access to general practice care; this is being modified now to allow for up to 1,000 salaried GPs to be employed through this scheme. The ARRS scheme is not popular with many GPs, for despite the extra staff being a 'free' asset to them, it takes a doctor or nurse considerable time and effort to supervise them, and ensure that no clinical problems are missed by these non-registered staff.

Health inequalities and population health
The average life expectancy for males in the UK is around 79 years for men and 83 years for women. This is double the life expectancy that was thought to exist in 1845! But there is a real gap in life expectancy of as much as 15-20 years, between people who are affluent and in work, and people who live in deprived communities. Those who are in the least deprived areas are more likely to look after themselves with a healthy lifestyle, and less likely to smoke, eat fatty foods and be sedentary. Those most at risk of these health inequalities include people from disadvantaged backgrounds and minority ethnic groups who are much more likely to have a mix of ill-health conditions, disabilities and/or severe mental illnesses, than the more affluent population. Cardiovascular diseases like atrial fibrillation, high blood pressure, high cholesterol, and chronic kidney disease account for a fifth of the gap years in life expectancy between people who are better off and those living in the most deprived communities.

Healthy life expectancy was around the age of 65 years in the early 2010s and is around that level now (though do note that this is an average four years lower than the population in Japan, where the majority of the population have healthy lifestyles). With the increased life expectancy these days, it does mean that many people living into their 80s and 90s, have chronic health conditions, so that their last few years are spent in poor health.

The 2.8 million people of working age who are off long-term sick, and the estimated extra 10 million people who are in work but have a limiting health condition, put considerable pressure on the NHS and welfare system.

The impact of the pandemic on the delivery of our health services across the UK is still obvious. That is, not only the effects of 'long' COVID that has been thought to affect up to two million adults and the increased numbers suffering from anxiety and depression, but also the disruption to the delivery of healthcare that is still ongoing, with a waiting list of more than 7.5 million adults in England waiting for agreed elective treatments in early 2024.

It is difficult to interpret statistics sometimes. Apparently, the prevalence of diabetes in 2008 was thought to be 5.1% (that's around one in twenty people), whereas in 2022 it was logged as 7.5%. But it could be that doctors and nurses are better at spotting and diagnosing diabetes these days, rather than yet more people have developed it? There's been a similar rise in the numbers of people recorded as suffering from high blood pressure, from 11.3% in 2004, to 14.4% in 2022; there has been lots of publicity about the dangers of a high blood pressure with frequent community events and projects to get people to be more aware that they should get their blood pressure checked – in churches, pharmacies, gyms etc. It looks as though people with long-term health conditions account for at least 50% of GP appointments, and 70% of inpatient bed days in hospitals. And as more than 14 million adults in England have already developed at least two health conditions and around 26 million people have at least one long-term health problem, there will continue to be a lot of pressure on NHS services in the foreseeable future.

We need to be planning for the future provision of the NHS if it is to grow and improve as it has done over the last 76 years to meet the needs of the population; one prediction is that the UK population will be likely to be about 82 million in 2070 (I'll have popped off by then), with 27% of these aged over 65 years old, compared with just 19% of our current population being in this age group.

Funding of the NHS

These days, the spend on the NHS budget in the UK is about 8.3% of GDP (gross domestic product) compared with around 2.8% of GDP around 70 years ago in 1955 soon after the NHS was created – though of course we have a much wider range of NHS treatments and services now. Health spending was devolved to Scotland, Wales and Northern Ireland in 1999, and comprises about a fifth of the overall UK health budget; being more in control, they have made their own decisions, such as not charging working age adults for NHS prescriptions, as we do in England.

The NHS is 99% funded from general taxation and National Insurance contributions, plus derives small amounts from patient charges for some specific services. About 60% of the NHS budget is used to pay for staff, around 20% pays for medication and other supplies, with the remaining 20% divided between the costs of premises, equipment, training, medical equipment, cleaning and catering.

The current NHS budget sounds a lot, with around £160 billion being allocated in England for 2023/ 2024. A considerable amount of funding gets wasted each year on 'projects', like the seven 'Nightingale' hospitals which were created to help cope with the influx of patients with COVID in 2020, at a cost of over £500 million, but were barely taken up. As many poorly thought out governmental schemes for the NHS are imposed without reasonable consultation with clinicians and the public, many of these go on to be substantially underused. Unfortunately, a good deal of funding needs to be spent on NHS estates such as hospitals; as these age they require a good deal of updating and investment to be able to provide modern healthcare services. About a quarter of the 6,000 or so general practices in England are based in NHS premises – the rest are owned by the GP partners themselves, or private, third-party companies who then lease the building(s) back to the GPs. The NHS reimburses GP practice owners for the use of their premises by a cost-rent agreement. It's all very complicated!

There is hope that the NHS can empower the public to self-care through greater use of the NHS App, if it is recommended and used by NHS organisations and others. This should minimise funds spent on avoidable health conditions – if we're lucky!

Our workforce now
Around 1.4 million people work in NHS hospitals and community health services in England, filling about 1.25 million full-time equivalent posts. Over half (53%) are professionally qualified clinical staff, including all doctors and qualified nurses; with around 168,000 full-time equivalent (FTE) doctors who work in all NHS settings, of whom 35,000 work in general practice. Some of these GPs work part-time, so that's equivalent to 27,000 full-time equivalent roles - as GP partners or salaried GPs or GP locums or trainee. These workforce numbers are similar to those in social care too – with an estimated 1.6 million people being employed in the adult social care sector in England these days, with around a 10% vacancy rate. They care for people with physical disabilities, learning disabilities, physical or mental illnesses; and then there are thought to be nearly five million unpaid carers too.

The number of doctors is 33% higher than ten years ago. But, one calculation is that England has only 2.9 full-time doctors per 1000 population, compared to the EU average of 3.7 per 1000 population. The number of GPs has not grown at the same rate as the number of hospital consultants has, so nowadays there are nearly twice as many full-time equivalent consultants as GPs.

There are more than 333,000 nurses across the NHS in England, which is 21% higher than 10 years ago. Nearly two thirds of nurses work in adult and general care settings, with 12% working in mental health settings and 11% in community services. But there are far fewer district nurses and learning disability nurses these days compared with just 15 years ago.

A recent review of our NHS workforce with that in other comparable countries undertaken by The King's Fund showed that the UK has much fewer doctors and nurses compared to most other countries like Austria, Sweden, Germany, Australia; it relies heavily on foreign-trained clinical staff too. And we have to remember that many in our NHS workforce are ageing and will be nearing retirement soon, creating more pressure on the workload of those doctors and nurses left in post.

June, an academic nurse now, was thinking back over her career. 'Once it was, and it still is, a privilege to be a nurse' (she was a student nurse in

1984-87).' She wore her cap with pride, once she became a staff nurse on a hospital ward in the late 1980s. She then carried on training and was a practising midwife from 1990 to 2005. In that time period she noticed "dominating husbands or partners being present at the birth of their baby" and was puzzled how in the 1990s no-one noted the 'red flags' of possible domestic violence. She supported the women who chose to confide in her. June thinks that even now in 2024, NHS staff need to be more aware of potential domestic violence occurring even if the female patient does not talk about it; they need to say 'you don't deserve that', and advise the woman in a friendly way how to access help and support.

The numbers of clinical staff might seem to be increasing but we need many more to handle the escalating workload and soaring patient demand, especially with an increasing proportion of our population being over 60 years old and so more likely to develop health conditions, or frailty. There are currently at least 125,000 vacant posts in health and social care in England, so the NHS and social care use 'banks' of staff, and agency staff, to fill vacancies which cost us tax payers £billions more in staffing costs each year.

Other key NHS hospital workforce groups continue to grow, such as the now almost 18,000 professionally qualified ambulance staff, 12% more than in 2019 and over 81,000 allied health professionals, 20% more than in 2019.

International recruitment into the NHS workforce is growing. Most NHS staff in England are British and nearly 19% are known to have non-British nationality, the most common being Indian, Filipino and Nigerian. The numbers of NHS staff with a nationality other than British is higher for doctors (35%) than nurses (27%). In the last five years, the number of international graduates joining the medical workforce increased by 40% and almost half of new joiners to the nursing and midwife council register had trained overseas. The UK has become increasingly reliant on international healthcare workers, as staff came from countries such as the Philippines and India in the early 2000s and later from other parts of the EU, such as Italy, Portugal, Romania, and Spain. After the 2016 Brexit vote the focus seemed to switch back to recruiting NHS staff from non-EU countries such as India, Pakistan, Philippines, and Nigeria; for instance, in 2024, almost half of new joiners added to the nursing and midwifery council register, and thus actively part of the registered nursing workforce, were from India. EU nurses have not only stopped joining but have started to leave the NHS. Between September 2016 and 2021, the NHS lost 11,000 EU trained nurses, and gained 30,000 nurses from the rest of the world.

Last year almost 7,000 UK doctors applied for a visa to work abroad, with one in four going to Australia. One doctor who lives there now relayed: "It had never been my plan to become a doctor and move to Australia. After graduating I worked for three years as a junior doctor. Then, in 2015, when I was 27 years old my boyfriend (now husband), who's also a doctor, was offered a job in Melbourne. I followed him out here. Western Australia is launching a programme to recruit 31,000 British doctors. One of the big draws is the money. A junior doctor can earn about 50 percent more. Consultants in Australia earn an average of £150,000 a year, as opposed to about £100,000 in the UK, and they can be paid overtime too. Here I work four ten-hour shifts and have three days off. Despite this, my British colleagues over here feel a lot of guilt. We've come out here for a better way of life and an improved work-life balance, but the trade-off is that we miss our families a lot."

As pressures rise on those NHS staff remaining in post, work-related stress, moral injury, and burnout within the workforce are very common. Statistics show that sickness absence rates have been increasing, with for example the average number of sick days in hospitals nowadays being around 6.4 days lost per doctor and up to 20 days per nurse per year. A recent national survey revealed that these days about one-third of NHS staff report that they feel burnt out because of their work, and even more find their work to be emotionally exhausting; which overspills into their off-duty time and family lives. Just as in the old days, in the 1970s, a *resident* hospital doctor (the new name for a *junior* doctor as from September 2024) might find they are covering 100 or more patients on hospital wards if other doctors are unexpectedly off sick or on annual leave; then they end their shift late and very stressed because they stayed on working unpaid extra hours in line with their medical conscience. Even if agency staff or locums are brought in at very short notice this can create extra pressure if they are unfamiliar with the clinical and management protocols, or site, that they have been allocated to work in at short notice.

David had such a great experience of using the NHS that he recently relayed his story and his thanks to the wonderful staff who looked after him, in my local newspaper. He had woken up at home with chest pain, so phoned 111. They quickly responded and listened and an ambulance then took him to A&E. By 9am he was transferred to the Ambulatory Emergency Care department where he was assessed and admitted to a cardiac ward with suspected unstable angina, about 8 hours after arriving at A&E. The following day he had two stents inserted into the blood vessels of his heart; and was then sent home. He really praised the way that every member of staff he met in the hospital seemed to care; and that their passion and team spirit was spread widely to include the patients too.

If we want to retain newly qualified doctors and other registered staff then we need to think of a smart idea like cancelling student loans accrued by any health professional over time, ensuring that they are motivated to remain working in the NHS and feel that their contribution is valued. Dr Gabby, a resident doctor described how she paid for her university tuition fees for the first four of her five years training (fifth year 'free') ie £9,250 per year and an annual £4,200 student loan. She not only needed to pay to rent a room and utility bills such as heating as a medical student, but also required a car to travel in her last two years as a medical student as some hospital and community placements were many miles away from her university and the placement hours included evenings and weekends. She accrued an £80,000 debt over her five years as a medical student despite some handouts from her parents; and that debt has high ongoing interest rates (currently 7%).

How's general practice care doing?
General practice is in crisis. It appears to be grossly underfunded, stretched beyond its capacity and providing more complex patient care these days, so that the morale of GPs and their teams is low. People are more likely to consult their GP these days, compared with 1995; then there was an average of 2.5 consultations per patient per year, as opposed to an average of five consultations per patient per year now,

30 or so years later. GPs in the UK provide around one million consultations per day taking an average of 9.2 minutes, and patients commonly present with as many as three separate problems (though it is common for these to be linked by the GP in a way that often the patient did not previously understand was the case). A recent report confirmed that nearly half of patient consultations were delivered on the same day as the booking was made and 70% were provided within seven days of the person booking it.

Mary's patient story is a great example of how patient-centred general practice still is, with GPs determined to do the best for their patients. Mary (aged 60 years old) works in a pub in a dual role as a cleaner and floor server, both very active roles. As a long-time smoker she had been diagnosed with COPD. When she had 'flu like symptoms and was very short of breath last winter, she phoned her practice and got a face to face appointment the same day, when she was given steroids and antibiotics. She was reviewed one week later and got a second course of each medication. Although she was unwell still, Mary felt that she must return to work as she couldn't manage on state sick pay. As she was VERY short of breath still her manager sent her home. She again phoned her GP and saw him the same morning. This time he sent her to A&E to be reviewed. She only waited an hour before having a chest Xray - which had no sinister findings, except a left sided chest infection. Mary was offered admission but insisted on returning home as her children live nearby and were happy to look after her whilst she took a third course of antibiotics and steroids. This time the medication beat the infection and Mary was happily back at work two weeks later, able to work without being short of breath. The good news is that she's now quit smoking for six months after that scare and the in-depth advice and encouragement the teams of doctors and nurses have given her throughout her general practice and hospital care.

General practices in areas with the highest levels of deprivation have on average 300 (14.4%) more patients registered per GP than practices with the least deprivation. And of course, patients living in socioeconomically deprived areas have multiple health needs compared to those in more affluent areas. On average, as of 2024, there were 2,294 patients per full-time GP in England - around 20% more patients per GP than in 2015 and about 7% more than in 2019. A GP typically allocates ten minutes per patient appointment, whereas doctors in other countries with similar roles may go up to 25 minutes a patient as a norm; GPs in the UK are aware that 10 minutes is not always enough to undertake a safe, high quality consultation, so they often run late with their surgeries, putting their own time in. There just aren't enough GPs to extend the length of their patient consultations – things need to change with many more doctors being urgently needed to reduce the dangerously high workload of GPs.

The total number of general practices in England dropped by around 20% ten years on from 8,044 in 2013 to 6,419 in 2023. The average practice list size in 2023 was 9,724 compared to 6,867 in 2013. The number of GP partners is declining too; partners account for just 53% of the GP headcount – the rest are employed as e.g. sessional GPs. People think that GPs earn an extortionate amount for the job they do. That's not true. I looked up the earnings of doctors working at a local general practice as relayed on their website – selecting that practice at random. The average pay for a full-time GP who'd be working for around 45 – 50 hours a week probably, with many other hours spent on related work such as preparing for appraisal, keeping up to date reading academic journals etc, was £78k last year, before tax and National Insurance and professional fees were extracted. Quite a lot less than train drivers earn from what I've read recently in the news! And the national funding available to GPs to run their practices as small businesses is plummeting too, so that the 'expenses to earnings ratio' for GP partners is increasing; some think that the current arrangements for squeezing of funding is putting the existence of general practices under threat, and our independent general practices may not survive much longer.

A GP typically spends about three-fifths of their working time on direct patient care these days, seeing patients in person or remotely; with about 10% of their working hours allocated to administrative tasks and the rest spent on indirect patient care – writing referral letters, arranging hospital admissions, attending meetings, updating or individualising clinical protocols, undertaking continuing professional development and much more. GPs intend to go home by 6.30pm, but some get kicked out by the cleaners leaving at 7.30pm. It's common then for GPs to click on and do the rest of their administrative tasks and follow up emails etc from home – maybe working on these until 10.30pm!

A local practice in a deprived area near to me for example, has a patient list size of 11,900; with four GP partners who do six sessions a week on three days plus four salaried GPs who do a mix of four to seven half-day sessions; the full-time practice manager, several practice nurses including an advanced nurse practitioner, and some of the new 'additional roles reimbursement scheme' staff funded by Primary Care Networks – a full-time physician assistant, full-time paramedic and part-time clinical pharmacist; as well as other non-registered staff such as healthcare assistants and receptionists and administrators. Succession planning is all about the nature of the whole team and the skill mix- not just about the GP partners these days.

Paula, a practice manager was reminiscing about the team culture that existed in the 1990s until 2012 or so. In those days, health visitors, district nurses, community psychiatric nurses, physiotherapists, chiropodists and phlebotomists were all based in her practice; the Trusts who employed them paid marginal rental for the space for them to be based there to deliver usual care to the patients registered with the practice and others nearby. All of these staff were moved out about 10-15 years ago; with health visitors being the last to leave. This separation initiated the disintegrated primary and community care that exists nowadays. So, Paula's daughter Alice has only seen a health visitor once in the five years since her birth; whereas Florence (aged 8 years old) saw a health visitor when she was 7 days old and regularly thereafter – for regular weigh ins, vaccination reviews etc. This means too that children with disabilities such as autism may be missed in their early years.

Every successful general practice needs a great practice manager who will take responsibility for finance and payroll, and manage staff well in constructive ways so that the GPs and nurses can get on with providing the clinical care. The income from the various bureaucratic streams can be a challenge. The Quality & Outcomes Framework (QOF) requires the practice manager to support and supervise practice staff to prioritise the attainment of indicators, even if this is not the most important part of their clinical delivery. Data quality facilitators used to come into a practice and help with auditing the achievements ready for the QOF deadline, but they are no longer allowed to do so. The Impact and Investment Fund (IIF) can be difficult to access if included targets are not acceptable to patients e.g. if parents don't agree with baby immunisations. Local quality indicators and attainment targets are often not set until July - so that leaves only eight months or so to call patients in for a review and get them started on improving their health targets (like good blood pressure control).

> THE DOCTOR USED TO SHAKE YOUR HAND BUT NOW IF YOU PUT YOUR ARM OUT THEY PUT A BLOOD PRESSURE CUFF ON IT.

> THEY MUST GET PAID FOR EACH CHECK THEY DO.

The team spirit and mutual support is still there in many general practices: a practice manager recently described to me how he admires the older doctors who came out of retirement to help with the COVID crisis: "They're good at putting patients at ease, and enjoy their role, relaying that job satisfaction" he said. And in another practice Dr Fiona who's been working as a medic for nearly 40 years is still proud to be a doctor "I love my job" and she still socialises with nurses, doctors and trainees in her team and recently organised a barbecue supper in her garden for 30 of the practice team.

There are lots of good examples of how well the clinical pathway from GP to hospital care works, if a patient is thought to be likely to have a serious health problem like cancer. The aim is for anyone suspected of cancer to be seen by a hospital medical expert within 14 days. For Ann this was even faster. She had felt a lump in her breast and decided to phone in to book an appointment with a GP – and she saw the doctor face to face the next day. That then led to the GP referring her to the hospital and she attended the breast clinic 10 days later. The biopsy they took then and there showed that she had a benign tumour, which was not cancerous. She still needed follow on care as the scan showed that the lump was comprised of two cysts; and she was warned that they might merge to one large cyst and that could cause some complications. They were consequently removed two days later! What a fast and competent service!

Another good example of how well GPs and hospital specialists interact in the care they provide comes from Bob. He was diagnosed with ulcerative colitis in his 30s and was shocked to find that he had bowel cancer when aged 48 years old - but he has lived to tell the tale five years later. Bob says that his treatments and the NHS care given to him for the last 20 years have been 'life saving' and is clearly very grateful for all the efforts in looking after him. When Bob noticed blood in his poo five years ago, it took around 14 days from reporting his symptoms to his GP until his diagnosis and then within three months he'd had his major bowel operation and started chemo treatment. Bob was given multiple options for a range of treatment by his doctors along the way, and he feels that he was fully informed to make the right decisions throughout his experience with the NHS. Bob also praises the care and support that he was given by the NHS following on from his operation and says that he got around one year of after-care and that "everyone in the NHS has been brilliant".

And hospital care?
Hospital care is very stretched too. Recent statistics show that in summer 2024 more than two million people in England were waiting for an agreed procedure in hospital; and 300,000 of these had been waiting for over one year, and 10,000 of these for more than 18 months.

These long waits for acute hospital care are replicated in mental healthcare too; for instance, in Spring 2024, 345,000 people were waiting more than one year after their initial referral, to be seen by a mental health team.

A&E departments seem very popular, but maybe that's because getting a GP appointment can prove difficult! In the three months period over summer 2024, there were nearly 7 million attendances at A&E in England. The staff managed to admit, discharge or transfer 76% of those attending within four hours – so hopefully reducing the strain on those waiting for care, on beds in hospital corridors. Let's hope this great work ethic of the A&E staff continues over the winter and the range of doctors' strikes are now discontinued.

There are so many good examples of the care provided in A&E. Simon aged 4 years old recently went with his mum Clare to A&E as he had a sore throat and a bit of a temperature and she was worried that these were symptoms of 'Strep A' which she'd seen that some young kids had died from, on the TV news that morning. They were in and out of the hospital within an hour with a negative diagnosis for Strep A – as the A&E doctor reassured them that it was just a normal viral throat infection that Simon had, and he did not need any antibiotics. Simon's Mum was not criticised by the A&E team for wasting their time – they could see that Clare thought it could be a medical emergency because of the stories on TV, and that her unnecessary visit to them was justified. If A&E were much more stringent about who could visit them and why, there'd be lots of missed medical emergencies resulting in avoidable deaths or severe illnesses.

And at the other end of the age spectrum, Nigel was telling me that he had recently taken his elderly father Dan (aged 86 years old) into A&E after he reported dropping a heavy object onto his foot; he already had metal rods and screws in that foot due to prior foot surgery. His father was checked in by the A&E team within five minutes of their arrival at hospital and only had to wait for a further 10 minutes or so before being seen by a doctor, despite the hospital being very busy that morning. Dan was sent home without the need for any further hospital treatment with advice on how to self-care and relieve the inflammation caused by his minor injury. Nigel remembered the hospital staff being really polite and kind and felt they'd been "very lucky".

Tim relayed his father's recent experience of emergency care. His father Carl is aged 93 years old and when his wife died 18 months ago, he moved to a care home soon after. When he coughed up 'black stuff' the care home staff called for an ambulance and alerted Tim who joined his father on the trip to hospital. The ambulance took just 30 minutes or so to pick them up. Carl was put on a bed in a hospital corridor that was set up as a ward. Bloods were taken there and he was reviewed by a doctor and cared for by a nurse. He was admitted to a side room on a proper ward at 3pm. MRI scans were done and nothing serious requiring an acute intervention was found, so there was no need for Carl to stay in hospital overnight. The decision to discharge Carl was made at 7pm and as an ambulance wait would have been three hours, Tim drove him back to his care home in his own car. The hospital nurses were very helpful in enabling Carl's transfer – they sourced a wheelchair and stayed with him whilst Tim retrieved his car from the car park, and drove to pick up his father from the hospital entrance.

So many patients are lying on trolleys in corridors, waiting to be admitted to a hospital ward or discharged to their home or elsewhere. The CQC found that only two in five people are able to leave hospital when they are ready to do so. The length of stay in hospital increases with a person's age; patients under 75 years old have an average length of stay of 3.4 days, while the average for patients older than 75 years is 8.6 days. Up to 14,000 beds in hospitals in England are thought to be occupied by someone who is clinically ready to leave. Staying in hospital longer than they need can lead to them having an increased risk of infection, worsening mobility and plummeting mental health.

A senior hospital manager recently updated me that the ward staffing ratio should typically be one nurse caring for eight patients during day time, with a one nurse to twelve patients ratio for night time shifts. But it can still be difficult to provide safe and effective care if two nurses need to attend to one patient, if for instance that patient has an allergic reaction and there are no spare nurses standing by! If a nurse is off sick at short notice the nurse/patient ratio may reduce to 1:16 patients that day.

A hospital nurse I was talking to recently said where she works: "We've wards where there's two nurses for 32 patients- and those patients can be extremely poorly. We just can't cope."

Nowadays a resident doctor's typical day on a hospital ward starts at 8.30am and finishes at 4.30pm with a handover to evening staff who work 4.30/5pm-9.30pm and then night staff who work from 9pm-9amish and handover to those starting at 8.30am. A resident doctor usually works an average 48 hours per week in a hospital role with a basic salary of about £40k, reflecting the higher hourly rate for night shifts. This is an exhausting work life, so resident doctors try to leave on time if they can, unless urgent patient care must be prioritised. Resident doctors are often moved round between teams too, to cover for staff who are on holiday or off sick, so that means a lack of continuity of care for patients who have different doctors everyday looking after them on the hospital ward, and destroys the team culture that used to be the lifeline that kept doctors going on pressured days.

Another factor in today's NHS staffing and safety levels for patient care is the pattern of workforce delegation that is common today. Nowadays, nurses working on hospital wards do the admission paperwork as patients arrive which doctors used to do, including rating the patient's risks, such as of falls, nutrition, dementia etc. Nurses now give out medication by mouth or intravenously. Healthcare assistants now take patients' biometric observations such as blood pressure readings or blood oxygen saturation levels at regular hourly reviews instead of nurses. Dr Paul was describing the more senior responsibility that a nurse routinely takes now that a doctor would have taken a few years ago: "If a patient comes to A&E with a suspected heart attack, they can be assessed by a specialist nurse, who can admit the patient or send them home if they do not think they actually had a heart attack and their symptoms were due to a less serious problem like indigestion." So, the patient does not necessarily see a doctor these days.

As a resident doctor on a cardiology ward Dr Paul describes much of his working role being spent on non-face to face care such as writing discharge letters, being very careful to document everything that has occurred and that matters. Once he's finished that discharge letter the hospital pharmacist checks and edits it further. The hospital ethos is to 'get the patient out' – so a resident doctor must prioritise any patients who can be discharged, unless another patient is critically ill and needs urgent medical help.

Doctors, however senior and whatever their clinical specialty are still in the main, patient-friendly and will put themselves out to provide the care that patients want. A great example that a friend told me of recently is of her son, Adrian (aged 32 years old) who had NHS funded surgery on his knee last year. He was gradually improving and wanted to start running again. His orthopaedic surgeon had discharged him a few weeks previously but had said that Adrian could always ring him if he wanted advice in future. So, Adrian gave Mr M a ring on the personal phone number he'd shared, and he answered straightaway. 'Come and see me in clinic on Friday' he invited Adrian – and so he turned up at 9am at the hospital as arranged, and got some great reassurance and support from Mr M – and started his first run that same afternoon. Not so good for the patients in booked appointments though that morning with their extra 10 minutes wait, as Adrian had been added in!

Providing great children's care is very challenging. Hospital teams need to interact with general practice and community teams usually, before and after their inpatient hospital episode. Chatting with Kitt's parents recently I realised what 'integrated care' means in real life. Kitt was born in 2022 and his abnormalities were detected in a scan at Royal Stoke University Hospital when his mum, Becky, was 34 weeks pregnant.

This immediately generated interactive working between the obstetric staff at Royal Stoke and in Liverpool where Becky had a specialised scan that triggered an emergency caesarean section. When Kitt was born with no linking oesophagus between his mouth to his stomach he was admitted as an emergency for intensive paediatric care at the Alderhey Children's hospital in Liverpool. There he had a surgical operation to reattach his oesophagus which was successful. Whilst Kitt was in hospital for over five weeks, his parents, Ben and Becky, stayed free at the associated hospital hospice for relatives of child inpatients who were having palliative care, or were seriously ill. The teams of hospital nurses and doctors who cared for Kitt all wore various colours of scrubs which indicated their work roles and made it much easier for parents to understand if they were interacting with a surgeon, nurse, urologist, psychotherapist or dietitian. Kitt's parents were very impressed with the hospital after care. They were allowed to take part in deciding when, or whether, Kitt should have follow on surgery. They asked the doctors to postpone the proposed stoma surgery when Kitt was 9 months old, that the Liverpool hospital team were planning to do, and they took part in an arranged video call three months later with five other clinicians in the room. Becky and Ben talked through their reservations about Kitt having surgery and how it might affect his spine and gut throughout his childhood. He's still on the waiting list...for when everyone agrees it is the right time to do further surgery.

Some good news is that the NHS has extended and enhanced the services provided in hospitals over the last few decades with complex equipment like CT scans, new medicines and other treatments, and innovative surgical techniques such as via robot surgery for prostate cancer and other intricate medical conditions. This has generally improved the clinical outcomes for individual patients, and reduced the time they spend in hospital, occupying beds.

And community services?
Community health services are stretched too. The organisations that provide NHS-funded community services are a wide range of acute, mental health, community and combined NHS Trust, community interest companies, private providers, local government and the third sector. There can be substantial delays in discharging patients from hospital to community services or to the patient's own home.

Millions of adults in England have failed to get an NHS funded dental appointment in the last few years. Only about one-third of NHS dental practices are accepting new child or adult joiners. Many people have given up trying and their teeth are rotting, as they can't afford privately funded dental care.

These days many pharmacies are closing, across the UK. NHS funding of pharmacies has dropped significantly, by about 30% in real terms since 2015. Only one-third of pharmacists working in community bases are qualified to prescribe medication, like doctors do; though when pharmacists qualify from 2026 they will have been trained to do so as a norm as part of their university course. These days, there have been problems with pharmacies having enough stocks of some drugs too, so that their customers sometimes have to go to a different pharmacy to access the medication prescribed for them.

Public health?
The *Health and Social Care Act* that was passed in England in 2012, transferred the responsibility and funding for providing public health services from the NHS to local government. So, from then on, Councils have been responsible and have experienced cuts to their public health budgets over the years, which has had ramifications on the scale and quality of services available. Public health teams are still instrumental in pushing for the adoption of the prevention of ill-health at scale, encouraging people to stop smoking, exercise more, eat healthily, take precautions to avoid sexual diseases, and some early years care provision. But unfortunately, ever since the responsibility and the £millions of funding for public health were transferred to local authorities, it has become increasingly disengaged from the central NHS delivery of care – in general practice and all other health settings.

What about social care?
Providers of social care are having a hard time. It has a stretched workforce, and I read recently that there are around 131,000 vacancies in adult social care in England. Many people complain that they don't get the range of social care that they need. Many providers of social care are based in the private sector; some delivering domiciliary care with staff who are on zero-hours contracts. So, there is a high workforce turnover when staff get fed up and leave.

The national edict which has just been shared by the Minister of State for Care, is to focus on improving 'service resilience' ready for winter by sustaining a 'home first' approach to support people to 'live independently for as long as possible', with close involvement of staff with service users, and their families and carers, who are receiving care. Nothing new there then!

Ambulance services?
There seem to be fewer ambulances available for emergency help these days, than are needed. When people call for immediate help from an ambulance for a person in cardiac arrest for example (described as 'Category 1'), the expected result is that the average pickup time is 7 minutes, though currently it is 8.2 minutes. If the call is for someone with a stroke or heart attack (termed 'Category 2') then the average response time is 32 minutes with 90% of calls seemingly responded to within 62 minutes. If the ambulance is called for a serious issue such as an older person who has had a fall (defined as 'Category 3'), the average response time is around 2 hours with 90% of the ambulances called arriving within 4 hours 45 minutes. Oh dear!

A paramedic told me the other day about how it was last winter when the ambulance queue outside the local hospital could last for more than eight hours! He might then spend his entire 8 hours shift in the same ambulance with one patient. Agency staff (an expensive option!) were then employed by the hospital to triage patients waiting in ambulances to try to speed up the A&E reception process. That helped somewhat.

Service user satisfaction?
A recent report by the Nuffield Trust describes overall public satisfaction with the NHS as falling to 24% - with 52% reporting that they are 'dissatisfied' - the lowest levels since the survey started up decades ago. The main reason why people are dissatisfied with the NHS is the waiting times for GP and hospital appointments and staff shortages. Of those describing being satisfied with the NHS, this was because they valued NHS care being free at the point of use, and the quality of NHS care, services and treatments provided. If respondents described themselves as *frail* or *disabled* they tended to rate their experiences of hospital care lower. And, whilst 13% of respondents were satisfied with the social care they had experienced, 57% were dissatisfied.

Are we integrating the delivery of health and care now?
My husband Chris has recently had an early stage cancerous 'thing' removed from his scalp. He seems to be under three specialty teams at the hospital: dermatology, cancer and plastic surgery care; with his

follow-up wound care unevenly divided between the nurses and doctors in the hospital and his general practice. Great care, but discontinuous.

Following the passing of the Health and Care Act in 2022 in England, 42 new Integrated Care Systems (ICSs) were formalised as legal entities with statutory powers and responsibilities for planning and commissioning most NHS services in their area, collaborating with partners from local government, voluntary/ community and social enterprise sectors, NHS organisations and others to deliver health and social care for local people with some shared priorities. Population sizes vary from half to three million people, with varying numbers of local authorities and provider organisations. The ICSs' key aims are: improving outcomes in population health and health care, tackling inequalities in health outcomes, service users' experience and access to care, enhancing productivity and value for money and helping the NHS to support broader social and economic development. So, this goes beyond just treating sickness, to include a shift to prevention by tackling the causes of ill health too such as employment, the environment, and housing issues.

ICSs are aiming for better data interoperability within, and between, their partner organisations. But there's one huge problem, general practices and community pharmacies within primary care, hospitals and social care operate with different computer systems, making it extremely difficult for all to work seamlessly together without shared access to patients' care records and the latest information about their illness or wellbeing, if computer systems don't speak to each other and so disrupt individuals' whole-person, continuity of care.

Modernise the delivery of healthcare?
In 2019, the government introduced the additional roles reimbursement scheme (ARRS) in England to grow capacity, alleviate GP workload and help solve the workforce shortage in primary care. Initially intended to cover five new roles, the scheme has grown to include over 15 roles, such as the: clinical pharmacist, pharmacy technician, social prescribing link worker, health and wellbeing coach, care coordinator, physician associate, first contact physiotherapist, dietitian, podiatrist, occupational therapist, nursing associate, trainee nursing associate, community paramedic, mental health practitioner, advanced practitioner, general

practice assistant. The budget for the ARRS was over £1.4 billion in 2023/24 but the extra staff were not enough on their own to reduce the pressure on GPs' own workload – and in some cases added to it in the short-term. Recruitment through the ARRS has been strong, and currently stands at 29,000 additional clinical and non-clinical staff in general practice. Staff are providing additional appointments, improving patient access to general practice, and providing personalised, proactive, care for the populations that they serve. BUT there have been unanticipated consequences; more time than expected has had to be allotted for GPs to supervise the ARRS staff in some cases, so that then reduces the number of GP appointments available. With 8,000 or so pharmacists joining the ARRS scheme, that has drained staff from community pharmacies and acute hospitals that now have many vacancies for pharmacists. And this shift of healthcare professionals to working in general practice has meant that there are fewer new job offers for GPs, and some trained GPs are unemployed, even though there is a dire need for them to stay in work providing patient care.

Regulating thousands of medical associate professionals will help increase their deployment on the frontline as physician associates (PAs) and anaesthesia associates (AAs) to support doctors and surgeons in providing medical care and anaesthetic services to patients. With over 3,500 PAs and 160 AAs working in the NHS already, regulation will enable them to play an increasingly important part in supporting the workforce. PAs and AAs undergo two years of postgraduate studying on average. PAs deliver health care and treatment to patients, such as diagnosing illnesses, performing diagnostic and therapeutic procedures and developing treatment management plans, under the supervision of doctors, whilst AAs generally work in hospitals and emergency environments and provide care for patients before, during and after their operations or procedures. The government's ambition is to increase training places for AAs and PAs, with 1,000 more PAs being trained each year from 2023 to 2024 and 250 more AAs being trained each year from 2024 to 2025.

Dr Andrew thinks that "the newly invented associate roles that are thought to be able to replace registered nurses/doctors are not working. The scheme does not save any time for a doctor in delivering patient care and it creates more confusion as a GP or nurse or anaesthetist has to step in anyway, after a patient has been seen by an associate member of staff."

Work with private healthcare providers in as far as it benefits the NHS
It's confusing isn't it! A private hospital is sometimes commissioned by the NHS to provide extra operations and other in-depth care to patients to clear extreme back logs in local NHS hospitals. Those patients do not pay for their operation or stay.

General practices are small businesses and the GP partners or owners must meet contract requirements. GPs are talking about how they might see private patients in their NHS premises; though at present they are only permitted to see patients privately if they are registered with another general practice. It is confusing, as GP practices have always been classed as 'private' businesses, before, and after, the NHS was created in 1948, and their NHS contract is their main source of funding still – as well as additional income from sources such as universities for providing training to medical students. But the current decline in funding for general practices as a proportion of the NHS budget is taking a toll- around one in five GP practices have closed or merged in the last ten years, despite the general population increasing substantially as people live longer and more people come to the UK.

But most of private healthcare takes place in private hospitals – there were nearly 900,000 admissions to private hospitals for treatment in 2023 according to the Information Network that tracks private treatment. Much of this take up is by people who are fed up with the ongoing hospital backlogs (people in England were waiting for around 7.5million NHS hospital appointments in the Spring of 2024 for instance) and do not want to risk their health deteriorating due to a long wait that they can avoid by going privately. About one-third opted to self-pay and the others were covered by private medical insurance that they had taken out. Popular diagnostic procedures or operations for those self-payers included knee replacements, inguinal hernia repair, hip replacement, cataract surgery, epidural injection, bowel colonoscopy, knee arthroscopy. If this reduces a wait for surgery by one to two years for someone in their 70s or 80s who can afford to pay up, you can see why they might choose to self-fund their healthcare, to have a more pain-free and active life rather than wait in pain and uncertainty.

People using private healthcare doesn't take as much pressure off the NHS as is mooted, when defending its existence. Most people who can afford and use private healthcare will be more affluent and so less likely to have poor lifestyle habits, like smoking or taking illegal substances, or being obese. Then they are less likely to have long-term health conditions too.

I do occasionally seek a private consultation with a consultant at our local private hospital. I'm not quite sure why. I think it's because otherwise I'd go to my GP who I know will refer me to that consultant for an expert perspective, and I suppose I'm speeding up my health review and not taking up a GP appointment unnecessarily. I've also taken up the advert sent to my home by a private company for a health check where I've had an array of blood tests to check if I've any health issues that I'm unaware of. The staff member who checked my blood pressure was obviously not properly trained as he took it incorrectly, before taking my bloods. I've always come out as 'perfect', though a similar range of tests that my husband took up detected that he was likely to have prostate cancer, and NHS follow-up confirmed this and generated the right cancer treatment earlier than he would otherwise have had it.

Me now

Even now after retiring as a GP six years ago - I still provide informal medical help to friends and people I meet with, on healthcare related projects that I'm still engaged with. For example, in the last year I've diagnosed shingles in the eye after a person had been fobbed off by a local pharmacist as a time waster; I've tied a large skin tag on another person's neck with thread - after a few days it looked gangrenous but it then dropped off. I've checked two people's blood pressure readings recently at their request to find that both were unduly high and they are now on medication from their GPs. During COVID times I stepped up to join the 'temporary emergency register' where I was reinstated as a practising doctor to help with the vaccination programme for nearly three years, and that helped to reduce local practice team workforce constraints, by liberating the staff to provide usual NHS care.

Please note: I have accessed many recent publications and reports to draw down facts about the NHS, the workforce, budgets and population health data in this chapter and for all the book. These often report conflicting content and so I've done my best to relay up to date information throughout.

Chapter 2. See, Do, Share – Dr Ruth's routes to fame

I began my academic work at Keele University in the late 1980s, alongside working as a popular local GP in Stone. One day I had seen a post advertised by the university for a 1.5 days per week contract for three years, for any interested doctor starting out in research. I'd been in my GP post at Stone for a few years by then and was starting to become a bit bored with doing general practice all day, every day during the week (with one half day off) and with a full 24 hours day on call every fourth weekend. So, I asked (I mean begged) each of my four GP partners to let me apply. They agreed that I could have a Wednesday off from doing clinical work in the practice if I was successful in my application, so long as I sacrificed my half-day off per week and they kept my 1.5 days pay from the university, to share in our GP partnership bank coffers. I then applied for one of the two start-up medical academic posts - and got it.

Having witnessed work stress affecting so many NHS staff since I'd qualified as a doctor and having seen so many clinicians burnt out by their job roles, I decided to focus on this as my new academic interest in developing my research career. I ended up doing a doctorate investigating the effects of work stress on doctors, and how doctors could sustain good health and wellbeing for as long as possible. There was widespread interest in the insights into doctors' stress that I had generated, as I shared my thinking and findings in a range of newspaper articles, and engaged with local and national healthcare organisations. I was awarded a General Practitioner Stress Fellowship by the Department of Health, based at the Royal College of GPs in London, for three sessions a week for two years in the mid-1990s, where I focused on extending my research and innovation work for my doctorate. I widened my focus to include medical careers in general practice and associated careers guidance too, with these national sponsors and further support from the West Midlands NHS Executive, including encouraging doctors to return to work after a career break and pushing for healthy working conditions in general practices.

When, after five or so years I presented my PhD thesis to Nottingham University, there was disagreement between the examiners about my approach and my findings, and my doctorate was rejected. I decided that, having spent so long doing the research, I wasn't going to let a few professors block my academic career, so I spent a further year evolving my research, and then submitted a revised thesis which was immediately accepted in 1995 and highly praised – so I had become 'Dr Dr Ruth Chambers'! I was already publishing my work in academic journals and starting to get recognition as a national expert on the subject. Sometimes you get setbacks, but you just have to pick yourself up and get on with things, so that your persistence pays off.

This was when I realised that if I was putting real effort into my research, then I needed to match that effort with sharing my learning and driving change. So, in 1996 I captured my messages for general practice teams in two videos on *Stress in General Practice: aggression and violence*, and *Stress in General Practice: management and prevention*, which both received a merit from the British Medical Association, creating widespread interest in my professional and academic circles. I resigned from my full-time GP role with the three sessions a week of academic work I'd squeezed in for a couple of years, to become an almost full-time Professor of Primary Care at Staffordshire University in 1996. I continued doing two GP sessions a week at another general practice in a deprived area to keep my hand in, and enable me to continue changing the focus of my medical career if, and when, I wished to do so in future. As a professor I organised various research and teaching projects, bringing a postgraduate medical focus to the university's School of Health, which until then was mainly focused on educating undergraduate nurses and undertaking nurse-related research and courses for practising nurses. With my academic paid working time, I also began my writing career, which has since seen me write or co-author over 80 books, mainly for healthcare professionals, but some for the general public too.

In 1999 I published my first two books: *What Stress!* for the general public and *What Stress in Primary Care!* – both published by the Royal College of General Practitioners. This led to real interest by other medical publishers too who approached me, and that same year in 1999 I had written two more books: *Survival Skills for GPs* and *Survival Skills for Nurses*, published by Radcliffe Medical Press based in Oxford, with a connected book *Opportunities and options in medical careers*, published the following year.

As my research into how work stress affected doctors in the 1990s became well known, and my educational resources on how to combat these work pressures and thrive featured in academic journals and newspapers, my expressions of interest in presenting at international conferences were grabbed. I've a map on a wall in my study at home capturing where I went tripping round the world as an academic. It's got flags pinned on all of the countries where I've presented at conferences or run workshops at other learning events. I started off presenting at UK events e.g. in Belfast, Edinburgh and London; but soon I was strutting my stuff at international conferences for doctors and nurses and others interested in healthcare and related topics across the world.

My academic work's taken me to America – Washington, Arizona, Naples, Miami, Fort Lauderdale; Canada – Vancouver, Toronto, Ottawa; Europe - Amsterdam, Madrid, Ireland, Lisbon, Florence; Scandinavia, Israel, Tunisia, Hong Kong, Japan and even more! I learnt quickly to be self-sufficient and guard against personal attacks out in the streets and avoid getting lost. I was determined to make the most of being abroad and enjoy learning about the local history or arts – getting out and about and not holing up in my hotel out of fear as many other delegates and presenters did who were attending these conferences, in unfamiliar locations.

Sometimes I would be at an international conference alone – then I had to learn to say 'no' very firmly to men propositioning me as a solo traveller and single woman, even as the decades went by. Sometimes I took my team along to a conference who'd helped with the research – and early on I learnt to include the costs of attending these high level conferences across the world in any grant funding I brought in – not just to cover my costs but also those of others involved at the university, or in an associated NHS organisation who wanted to come along to present our findings too. Starting out, I took my personal assistant Barbara to conferences in Israel and Ottawa in the 1990s – that gave her, her first experience of jetting off abroad from the UK. But she deserved it – she had spent ten years helping me with all the underpinning research work, maintaining databases, collating survey responses from research participants, helping to pull together graphs and evolve a set of Powerpoint slides.

The most prestigious international conference where I presented as one of the main speakers was in 1995 at an early stage in my academic career. I was flown business class to an international medical conference in Hong Kong – at their cost as I was an invited main plenary speaker on Doctors' stress, the main theme of the conference. As I was pretty new to the academic world, I knew no-one else from the various UK academic groups there, or from across the globe. I was very nervous about doing my plenary presentation- sitting on stage waiting to start talking to the 2,000 people in the audience with TV screens pitched around to showcase the speakers and our slides close up. I was third on and had to leave the speakers' stage whilst the second presenter was talking and rush to the ladies' loo some distance away with a burst of diarrhoea. I talked myself round in the mirror 'Come on Ruth- you can do it!' – then went back on stage and gave my talk in a confident seeming way to the packed lecture hall (and I wasn't incontinent of poo or words either!). That led to invites to many other international conferences in the 1990s/early 2000s -especially three annual conferences in America on doctors' health where I got to know Arizona, Naples and Washington pretty well! It was always a trial finding the right time to phone home and speak to my three kids and husband – balancing the nine or so hours time difference between the UK and USA location, and the bustling conference schedule – so I can remember trying to find times at around 10am 'there' time when the conference setting was ultra-busy, and trying to hear each of my family at home on a public phone in a buzzing venue (no mobile phones in those days to take to a quiet spot outside), where the time at home was about 7pm, after school and before the kids went to bed.

My last presentation at an academic event across the world was in Miami in 2019, at a supposed global nursing international conference. I had enough funding left in a project pot to take a team of four of us (covering travel, conference fees and hotel but not food and drink), from external investment in our digital upskilling of nurses to enable them to better deliver digital care. This was just before the COVID pandemic, when very few nurses in general practices or other health and care settings provided video consultations as routine care, or actively encouraged their patients to use health apps, or access their online medical records. We wanted to brag about how well our digital upskilling of nurses and other clinicians across England had gone, and how those taking part were nearly all using digital modes of delivery of care as a norm. BUT when we arrived (two days before the conference was due to begin so that we could get over our jet lag - oh and enjoy Miami of course!) we found that there were only 26 people attending the conference that we'd been led to believe would have hundreds if not thousands of nurses and academics present. We insisted on moving our various conference presentations to the first day, and then enjoyed another two days of holiday - free to explore Miami and visit the Hard Rock café, and sail around the coastline looking at the millionaire celebrities' second homes, whilst basking in the sunshine. We did get some refunds of our costs via PayPal, and I learnt that this was a well known scam – for people from Asia who were apparently presenting at a conference in America to get a travel visa to visit the USA, that they wouldn't have been able to get so easily otherwise.

I believe very strongly that you should allocate at least as much time and preferably more, in publicising and disseminating your research, as in the time you spend carrying out the studies. Too often research findings don't get heard about, except in very limited academic circles. Sometimes that's because the research takes so long to complete that it is out-of-date in our rapidly changing world before it can be published; other reasons include a novice researcher being unaware of how to overcome the many obstacles to getting published that includes the £2,000 or equivalent publication fees in euros or dollars that are often obligatory, and knowing how to pitch the research article to please the journals' reviewers so that they snap it up.

My dreadful experience of undertaking research as a medical student extracting fat samples from patients without their informed consent in 1973 (read more about this in Chapter 8), drove my interest in clinical governance over the years, when ethics and governance became 'must dos' by the time I undertook my doctorate research twenty years later. I became a local teacher on these topics as part of my Staffordshire University professorial role in the late 1990s, funded by the local health authorities in Staffordshire and Shropshire; then Radcliffe Medical Press, published a book on this topic that I wrote with a friend in 2000: *Making clinical governance work for you*. A couple of years later an academic dentist adapted our book content into a parallel book for dentists.

And then there was international interest too! The academic in Japan (Professor Yoshi) who had translated our book into Japanese and his colleague Professor Mori, invited me to do a speaking tour on clinical governance and ethics trotting around Japan in 2007 – and they covered all the costs. I did four presentations as an esteemed British academic – in Tokyo, Hiroshima and two other Universities. Of course, I took my husband Chris along to carry my bags to the conferences and on the train trips, on our all expenses paid speaking tour across Japan, never to be forgotten. Most of those in the audience could speak English, but there was always a translator standing beside me too. I've remained friends with Yoshi and Mori ever since, and they translated another book into Japanese that I had coauthored in English in 2018 too: *Making Digital Healthcare Happen in Practice: a practical handbook.* My long standing interest and focus on avoiding obesity and adopting healthy lifestyles has been weaved in and is obvious throughout this book – featuring as examples of using health apps or video consultation or online learning and more digital modes that health and care professionals can use in their delivery of care.

My main purpose in all of the work that I continue to do is to 'make a difference' – to improve quality of care, raise standards, enhance the health and wellbeing of people locally/ across the UK/ around the world! To help anyone who is interested and committed to improve the ways that health and care are delivered – by them, their teams and at scale. A few years ago in 2009, I with some colleagues, set up a quality improvement scheme for the then 60 or so general practices locally, across Stoke-on-Trent. This role was for the local Primary Care Trust, alongside my being a half-time GP partner at a general practice in a really deprived area of Stoke-on-Trent. We had some key foci for each general practice team, that included achieving quality indicators in their clinical work to extending the scope of the practice teams' provision of care – very wide-ranging. All practices were inspected by our NHS team and received individualised reports which detailed how they could specifically improve. The majority of practices scored well and received extra funds to recompense them for the time staff were allocating to the additional quality improvement of the care they delivered. But even in those general practices that did less well there were usually staff committed to providing good quality care, but who just needed help to reach those higher standards in their delivery of care. So, this whole quality improvement scheme was linked to education and support, rather than just harsh judgements, and was all about raising standards of practice, which was an aim that everyone shared. The evaluations year on year showed that general practice care across Stoke-on-Trent really improved despite the deprivation levels and local people's unhealthy lifestyle habits. With the help and encouragement of the local NHS boss, Graham, I successfully pitched for our local NHS to invest an extra £1.5million per year in the programme, improving the quality of care that the 260,000 or so patients registered with the 60 local general practices received.

This was allocated on a recurrent basis in 2009 and the arrangement lasted until 2022 when the Integrated Care Services Boards replaced the Clinical Commissioning Groups that had replaced the Primary Care Trusts (PCTs) and before that the Primary Care Groups (PCGs); the five Stoke-on-Trent PCGs were the NHS organisations who led on this with me in 2009 when I set up this Quality Improvement Framework (known as the QIF) programme. It worked!! Within three years many of the practices had improved the blood pressure control of their patients, for example. When we compared the statistics for what proportion of patients had well controlled blood pressure, the population data showed that Stoke-on-Trent had risen to be the fifth best out of the 17 PCTs across the West Midlands for blood pressure control for patients who also had other health conditions like diabetes; whereas comparative data in 2009 showed that they had the worst controlled patients of the 17 PCTs. Wow! We saved many strokes and lives with this programme, and extended the focus on many more health conditions, with higher clinical attainment targets over the subsequent years and those many quality improvements have extended and persisted at scale until this day.

My leadership and design of this pan-population quality improvement success was extended to other areas of Staffordshire too, albeit not in quite such comprehensive ways, without as much investment of funding and support and effort. But I think this was what jettisoned my being nominated for, and getting, an Order of the British Empire (OBE) honour for services to primary care in 2012. Nominating someone for honours is a fairly secretive process, especially when it is for an individual like me who was getting it for an outstanding achievement and not because they had run a national organisation and were stepping down, as is often the case. So, I don't know who exactly started the nomination process, and then spent hours inviting others who were aware of my work and respected it to also provide a supportive testimonial - it would probably have needed at least ten different supporters or even twenty. Friends tease me that OBE stands for 'Others' Bloody Effort' whereas the MBE, which is a slightly lower level honours awards, means 'My Bloody Effort' – but of course that's not true in my case!! I worked very hard to really get such positive changes to happen at a population level, using my networks, charm, determination, perseverance, time etc. etc. – of course I deserved the OBE!

My Day at Buckingham Palace receiving my OBE will feature in my fond memories forever (and the front cover of this book!). My father got an OBE too for his national achievements working on nuclear power, in the mid-1960s. So, the drive to make worthwhile changes happen at scale must be in my genes. I was lucky to ask for, and get, an extra visitor pass for all my immediate family to come along to the Palace ceremony with me, so that I didn't have to choose who wasn't to be invited out of my three children and husband. They each deserved a seat, having had to put up with my obsession with work that sometimes intruded into family time. The Royal College of General Practitioners very kindly provided a posh Daimler to chauffeur us from Euston station to the Palace; wait there for the two hours or so of the ceremony, then take us on to the Ritz which we had booked for a late lunch. It was a great experience. I was separated from my family who went on into the ceremonial hall, and sat waiting in reserved seats, listening to the Royal band who were dressed in smart uniforms. I was in a waiting room with the others who were receiving their honours and we were divided into groups from Lords and Ladies, Sirs and Dames, to those receiving a CBE, OBE and MBE. I became friendly with another lady, Jane, who was receiving her OBE in recognition of her national leadership on Sports; we hit it off as neither of us was wearing a hat and we were both dressed in smart, but not super-smart suits, and looking more natural. We queued up to be greeted by the then Prince Charles who was standing on the front stage – he told me I must deserve my medal if I was brave and determined enough to have achieved so much with such a challenging population as live in Stoke-on-Trent! Then once the ceremony was over we went off to the Ritz- we were pretty warm by then and my two sons aged in their early thirties took off their suit jackets as we sat down at our lunch table. One of the smartly dressed waiters was straight over and told them they'd have to leave if they didn't put their jackets back on, as they were too underdressed! It felt like we'd been warmly welcomed at Buckingham Palace, but scorned at the Ritz.

I've mixed with royalty (by personal invitation!) at Highgrove (both dinners hosted by Prince Charles) and Clarence House (it was really interesting seeing the Queen Mother's library of books and realising how normal she was) as well as those two invites to Buckingham Palace. I've attended work meetings in person at various key government buildings such as the Cabinet Office in Downing Street and private members' clubs nearby in London – all as part of ongoing projects or contributing feedback afterwards. But I'm just as happy mixing with local people at community events too - who are hard up, mixed up but terribly friendly and interested in my health projects and how it might actually help them.

One good example of mixing with the community came from my interest in what the pub sector might offer their customers, especially those who tried to avoid going to see their doctor and thus might have an irregular heart beat without being aware of it. If they did and it was diagnosed as atrial fibrillation (AF) then they'd most likely need blood thinning treatment to reduce their chances of having a stroke - which might be a very severe one from which they'd not recover or might die. With my increasing interest in technology enabled care in 2019, I led on a project to create an app that was based on virtual reality talks from a simulated doctor, nurse and patient as to how the viewer could take their own pulse or do a blood pressure check. The simulated doctor appearing on the app (who looked like me) provided interactive content about being aware of how important it is in a person's middle and older years to check their pulse, to find out if it has become irregular; in which case it might be that it is AF and they need treatment. We had the vision to create drink mats to signpost the app/QR code that could be scanned by customers of Wetherspoon's pubs to access the content and advice.
I emailed Tim Martin (now a 'Sir', then a 'Mr') who owns that pub chain across the UK (by guessing his email address, trying four versions and being successful with one of them!) and asked him if we could do this. He agreed (by email) almost straightaway and put us in touch with a

couple of regional managers. Within a week of putting the drink mats out on the tables of the 30 or so pubs across Staffordshire, the installation of our virtual reality app had rocketed, and we felt that we'd got our health messages out to the right people in an engaging way, with our use of virtual reality.

Another technology enabled care success that led to commitment from the top was with the use of Facebook. In 2016 we set up official Facebook pages for most of the then 80 or so general practices in Northern Staffordshire to relay health messages to their patient populations. We also helped individual nurses create closed Facebook groups for specific groups of patients e.g. to provide peer support for a range of maternity services including a dual focus on smoking cessation and obesity. A good result from our population messaging was the noteworthy increase in breast cancer screening attendance.

Over the previous ten years there had been a substantive decline in take up, locally and nationally. Uptake of breast screening improved by 13% in the local areas in North Staffordshire in 2019, where the mobile breast screening van service was located, with the local practice Facebook pages showing animations about the importance of breast screening to engage

women and minimize their fears. By the time we published our findings and insights the breast cancer screening team's official Facebook page had 1,682 followers and had attracted national interest as a useful communication tool for population messaging. We published an academic paper showcasing these findings too. I shared our successes with the top level clinicians like the lead nurse and medical director of Facebook based at their headquarters in the USA. They were very interested and keen to try and engage with politicians in England too. This ended up with the Facebook elite in Silicon Valley in the USA offering their London HQ for me to organize a national conference describing our experiences and successes of using Facebook for the delivery of health messaging and healthcare. Two of their senior leads flew over from America to join the conference and contribute as speakers and we also had a live plenary session with their medical director. The Facebook HQ team in London did all the hard work, collating the speakers' presentations, organizing the set up of the venue, providing free food and drinks for the 200 or so delegates (who did not have to pay to attend!) throughout the day.
It is a terrific venue and so hospitable – and the costs of the day were all absorbed by Facebook. I lost touch with their senior team after that – but that wasn't long before the COVID pandemic kicked in.

I'm often asked what my 'Secrets of Success' are. It's got to be about perseverance if you want to make a difference at scale, and being honest and credible to gain people's trust (not like a typical politician!). You need to recognise the contributions of others in your team; but if you recognise weaknesses in others then try to help them and don't berate or belittle them. You need to be creative, follow your ideas, and make things happen – don't ponder for too long. Remember too, 'If you don't ask…you don't get'!

My drive to make a difference at scale has led me to change the direction of my medical career from time to time. On one occasion, I resigned from the general practice where I was working (in Stone), without another job to go to, because I felt the work didn't challenge me enough. That's when I joined a team with the Department of Health looking into prescription fraud, which I felt was important, because NHS funds need to be spent on patient care, rather than lining the pockets of a few corrupt people, as I have described in Chapter 7.

We drew up a large number of recommendations which were put in place nationally and will have saved substantial amounts of money for the NHS. This experience taught me to question everything, to take nothing at face value, and think widely as to how the system could be misused. My general practice training in developing a problem solving/questioning approach makes you think of all possibilities, and stood me in good stead as the clinical lead on that national prescription fraud enquiry.

Another driver for me to be successful is that I really do want to help people. This may be patients, or work colleagues, or anyone with whom I come into contact. If you are genuinely interested in a person, they will respond differently than if you infer that they are just another person in the crowd. I've found that patients who've recently been discharged from prison are often treated as being inconsequential by the NHS – just left to cope mentally with re-entering the normal world. But if as their GP you are genuinely interested in how they are managing, so that they realise you really do care about their wellbeing, their self-esteem can improve, and they are more likely to consider improving their health and wellbeing in more constructive ways.

All people are important to the functioning of an organisation, and if people further down the chain of command are not respected, the whole organisation becomes a place where people don't want to work, and it is less successful. I think that leadership is about bringing out the best in people, and leading by consent and mutual respect. I value the admin worker or cleaner or waiter, as much as the chief executive. I often have meetings in local cafés. It generates far more creative discussions than being in the corporate setting of an office or via MS Teams meetings. The atmosphere is different - we laugh, poke fun at each other, but from those kinds of discussions come new ideas, and people realise that they can create better ways of doing things, perhaps think of others who could be involved, bringing in new dimensions.

So much of my work has come about as a result of the many grants and sources of funding that I've brought in. I've got better and better at pitching my bids and applications for likely £s. This determination to access external funds started as a medical student when I was very short of money as I did not qualify for a state grant because my father earned too much. But he had a mean streak and wasn't prepared to give me much to live on, over and above paying for my room - at first in the university and then out in the town. So, I entered and won First prize in a Vasectomy Association essay competition in my fourth year at medical school: Campbell R. *A review of the reliability and popularity of vasectomy* in 1974 (I was driven by winning £50 – a lot of money in those days, and not because this was a topic of interest!).

I successfully applied for a range of national and local funding and by 1999 I'd received a total of £300,000 or so grants for eleven various related programmes from the Staffordshire Family Health Services Authority, the Royal College of General Practitioners, the Department of Health, the Health Education Authority, the BUPA Foundation, the NHS Executive West Midlands region, and North & South Staffordshire Health Authorities. I got better and better at writing bids. When I totalled these grants all up recently, I realised that I'd brought in £6.9million from very many different funding sources between 2000 and 2024, all for projects and programmes that I was leading on where I was directly in control of how the funds were spent (in addition to the £millions that I'd successfully managed to get that were embedded as recurrent funds in system-wide quality services that became an NHS norm for Stoke-on-Trent practices, that were renewed annually for 12 years and still exist in an adapted format now)!! In the 1990s my funds were mainly centred on research into work stress and service improvement like the quality of medical audit carried out in general practices. Then I extended this to clinical audit of teenagers' contraceptive care; and facilitating clinical audit in prisons across Staffordshire, sharing that learning with a prison in Cheshire at their request. My research into work stress was funded by several grants focused on piloting an occupational health service for GPs as part of my national General Practitioner Stress Fellowship and comparing the health at work of doctors and teachers at the time. These included a focus on the effectiveness of a pilot occupational health service for general practitioners and a doctors' support scheme that I created and ran for three years with volunteer mentors befriending those doctors based in Staffordshire who sought help. When funding ran out I passed over the ownership and responsibility to our county-wide Local Medical Committee which is the sub-regional arm of the British Medical Association, who kept it going for a good few years.

I moved on to focus on medical careers and the need for career guidance and associated training in this for GP educationalists; establishing a re-entry scheme for doctors who'd dropped out of regular NHS work, and especially championing recruitment of GPs to inner city practices. I set up a very successful coaching scheme for GPs in the West Midlands alongside, to encourage the doctors who took up the offer, to sustain and expand their medical careers.

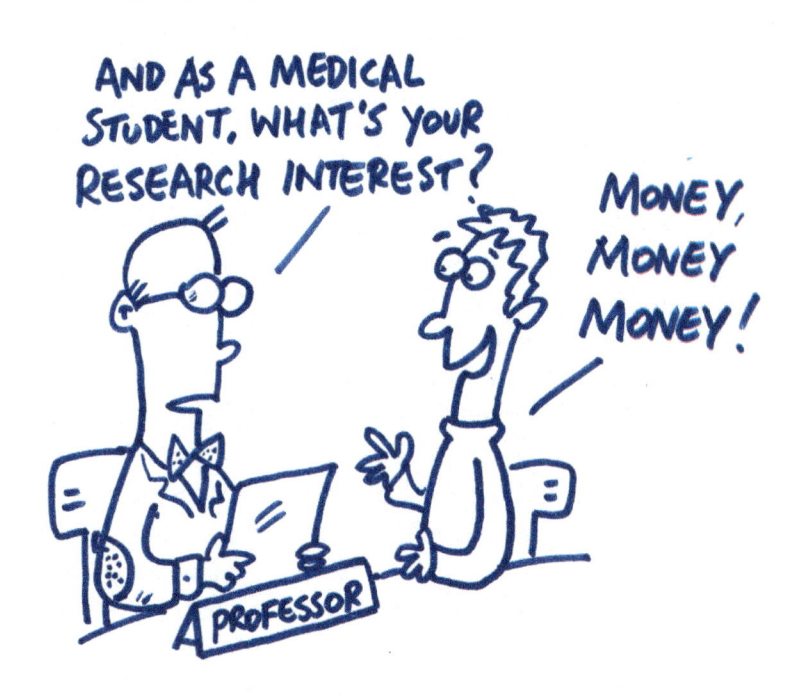

I extended my service improvement programmes to include the quality of care in nursing homes and how the GP's roles fitted in, as well as the follow-up care needed for patients with learning disabilities who had been discharged into a community setting. Then I progressed to a more generic focus on best practice in clinical effectiveness in NHS care and clinical governance, and how the perspectives and involvement of individual patients and members of the public fed into improving service design and provision.

I became more of a medical educator in the early 2000s, creating university and Royal College courses for teaching doctors (and dentists) to teach, research skills training, accredited professional development: basic and expert skills courses. If I focused on developing a programme such as *reducing teenage pregnancy*, then I would invariably write and publish an associated book – often including members of the project team as coauthors – in this case it was my daughter Steph, aged 14 years old then, who brought in the young person's perspective.

My interest in healthy workplaces expanded from the focus on overcoming work stress, to other matters such as *Back In Work* when I worked with the Department of Health to share good practice in preventing back problems at work, and promote good ergonomics. I still promote this subject now, using resources we evolved in that programme.

I extended my passion for education to aid the lower levels of administrators or managers or healthcare assistants or professionals in the NHS. Many of those I helped moved up the 'Band' scales of employment. This led to my extending my educational support to aid four refugee doctors whom I first met in 2004 – three from Afghanistan and one from Albania. Over the next 14 years I've managed to 'scrape' together around £400,000 from various NHS and Charitable sources to help these four doctors and a couple of others later on, to get to know our NHS system – temporarily employed as healthcare assistants in supportive local general practices, improving their English language skills and medical competence and capability to proven national standards, so that they all passed the series of national examinations to be recognised as fit to work in the NHS in the UK, to continue training in hospitals and general practice so that they could, and still do, practise as experienced, senior doctors here and now.

Another evolving interest was the prevention of health conditions and poor wellbeing and empowering individual members of the public to self-care, working as the clinical lead in the Department of Health's Working in Partnership Programme in 2005-2006 and evolving toolkits of best practice for general practice nurses and other clinicians working in primary care. I wrote an associated book on self-care and published related articles to share what we'd learnt with this national programme. I just received an accolade recently from the ResearchGate organisation that monitors the numbers of reads a published research article gets; apparently an article I'd written on *Supporting self-care in primary care* has just had 1000 reads from across the world which they've monitored – a great success. Sometimes ResearchGate updates me about how many researchers have cited a published academic paper that I've co-authored in their published research, and that can be as many as 30 citations of one of my research papers – by academics across the world based in the USA and Australia, but also Ghana, the Philippines, India, Sri Lanka and so on……..!

This push to get the adoption of self-care at scale became part of my focus on NHS sustainability and for instance, reducing hospital admissions using interactive text based, telehealthcare support. This was my first move towards the adoption of technology enabled care and in this case we focused on improving the management of high blood pressure (hypertension) in general practice, funded by the Health Foundation in 2012. Other funds for expanding our technology applications rolled in such as the national rollout of the Flo' telehealth service to general practice with the allocated national £496,000 funds held by my local NHS Stoke-on-Trent Clinical Commissioning Group in 2012-3. This was extended to support our team and other advocates of Flo' telehealth to join in as clinical advocates for telehealth for the NHS England/ Veterans' Health Association Washington programme (tripping over to Washington for a week or so, all expenses paid) with further funds of £50,000 allocated for 2013-5; and extended with a new focus on how telehealth could underpin integrated care and personalised care for people with long-term health conditions - attracting another £800,000 funding in tranches between 2014-2018.

My new interest in overcoming digital exclusion of citizens, and clinicians, took off in 2017 when I successfully bid to be part of the wave 2 programme led by the Good Things Foundation that allocated us £50,000 for a Stoke-on-Trent pilot. This was closely followed by NHS England allocating us £450,000 in 2018 for digital upskilling of general practice nurses via six action learning sets of ten or more nurses across Staffordshire and 12 more cohorts across England; then another £268,000 for seven more learning sets of practice nurses and four cohorts of social workers in 2019/2020. I had more time to focus on these innovative training programmes after I had stepped down as a practising GP partner from my practice in 2018. That so called 'GP retirement' didn't last long though, as I was back on the temporary emergency register within two years, to actively help with clinical practice in the COVID pandemic.

After that the funds kept rolling in for supporting technology enabled care services by creating digital transformation of general practices with various foci, such as wound care, spotting irregular heart rates in people not diagnosed with a related heart condition, improving the take up of pulmonary rehabilitation, and much more. When COVID hit I successfully applied to try out digital stethoscopes as part of novel remote care between nursing home settings and overseeing GPs. We also set up better facilities in, and associated learning resources with, 80 nursing homes across Staffordshire with a social enterprise company Redmoor Health to enable the staff to reliably enable video consultations with remote GPs, practice nurses or hospital clinicians, using a tablet placed on a trolley that could simply be moved to a resident's bedroom in the nursing or care home where they were living. Alexa deployment featured then too especially for isolated people living in the community and people who'd benefit from regular health messages like those with diabetes. Even now after retiring from my employed NHS role as a clinical lead for technology enabled care a couple of years ago, I've been able to attract funding from the local Council for aiding digitally excluded local people, and have recently set up a company, Raparu Consult CIC, with friends to retain my experience and to inspire and promote healthy living by empowering people to self-care and enhance their chances of living independently at home for longer.

As my career has evolved, I've captured my learning in articles in local newspapers, publications in academic journals, and in 83 books (so far!) for clinicians, academics, and the general public. A few of these 83 books that I've written are second, third or even fourth editions - when a first edition was found to be very popular with readers. A few have been translated into other languages for foreign readerships too – such as *Teaching Made Easy: a manual for health professionals* by Drs Kay Mohanna, David Wall and Ruth Chambers, which was translated into Korean in 2008; and クリニカルガバナンス *Making Clinical Governance Work for You* written by Chambers R, Wakley G, Yoshinaga H, Kobayashi S which was translated into Japanese in 2004 and published by the Japan Medical Planning group.

So, as you can see that my medical career pathway over the last 50 years has been pretty flexible and I've changed direction and focus many times, but then included my learning and interest from previous work experiences. I think that's kept me energised, even when juggling so many roles and responsibilities. Being a GP as my main thread has allowed me to be flexible in the range of other roles that I've taken on, and balanced against my frontline practice seeing patients on a daily, or weekly, basis alongside.

Chapter 3. Gender issues – across our NHS

As I was growing up, I had a good taste of the gender discrimination that I was to experience throughout my medical career. My Mum was our full-time housekeeper in charge of cooking, shopping and cleaning, who fitted in and obeyed my Dad's wishes (or I should say: 'instructions'!!). My younger brother Ian, was continually groomed and supported to meet my father's expectations of him – to excel at a private school (yes), go to Cambridge University (yes), become an important person (a doctor for 14 years, who then opted for a more academic life as a statistician). My parents did not expect much more from me than to replicate my mother's life story...and becoming a bank clerk was a suggested career path for me.

I started to grow my hidden rebellious nature as a teenager, to trick my parents into thinking that I was toeing the line so that they didn't confront me (or smack me!). I'd retreat to my bedroom – to escape from my father's critical eyes! He was very strict about the many hours of school homework I must do every day – but I didn't want to spend time doing that. I'd go to my bedroom and sit inside the door on the floor next to the radiator reading books of fiction, pretending to do my homework. Then when my Dad tried to storm in to check that I was studying, he couldn't open the door as I was sitting against it on the other side, pretending to keep warm. I had 20 seconds to switch my story book for my school work and then stand up to let Dad in to inspect my partly done homework.

In my day in the 1960s, a girl was not likely to go to university, let alone apply to study to be a doctor. Only around half of all girls at primary school passed the 11+ exam to get into grammar school. About a third of the girls who took 'O' levels (the equivalent of today's GCSEs) in my girls-only grammar school progressed to the sixth form. Very few of the sixth formers applied to university, even though there were no fees to pay in those days – and there was a state grant for students to live on, if their parents were not well off. I got good GCSE grades in English and history and pretty average in chemistry, physics and biology, and I wanted to do English and music 'A' levels. But my father said he'd only allow me to progress to the sixth form if I did science subjects; so there it was – I had to obey and study science 'A' levels, or try to get that job as a counter assistant in a bank.

I sat alongside a friend, both aged 17 years old, as we filled in our university applications. She was really sure that she wanted to do medicine – and listed six medical schools in order. I thought that if Sarah can do it- why don't I?; even though I didn't know any doctor, nor had I done any research into what medical schools offered. I just applied by location – away from my family- but not too far so that I could travel home as, and when. I listed two medical schools and pharmacy for the other options and just in case my 'A' levels were not good enough to get into university, I applied to an agricultural college too.

My family just laughed when I told them I'd applied for medicine. But I got an invite to Nottingham University for an interview for a possible medical school place. There was no support from my family for me to go for the interview and I had no smart clothes to wear, so I literally sewed my own skirt and a sort of jacket at home from a pattern I'd bought a few days before. I took three buses to get from my home to Nottingham as my mother wouldn't drive me (even though she had a car). I just about arrived on time and rushed into the interview. Somehow my self-determination appealed to them and I was offered a place, providing that I reached relatively mediocre marks in my three 'A' levels. Nottingham University was just setting up their medical school and was the first to recruit 30% of their medical student intake as female- the other medical schools in the UK in 1970 had a threshold of 10% for accepting women students. So, I got good enough 'A' level grades for me to be accepted to study medicine (phew!) and turned down my other offers for training in pharmacy at Loughborough or agriculture at Reaseheath College.

By the 1980s the intake of female and male medical students was 50-50 in most medical schools in the UK- now it is common for the majority of medical students in any one year to be female at all universities.

There was a noticeable lack of respect for female medical students then in the 1970s – from hospital staff and patients. For example, nurses wouldn't help me as a female medical student or junior doctor doing an obstetrics post, to sew up a vagina after a mother gave birth, whereas they'd be all over a male student or junior doctor aiding and abetting them. I learnt to do with two hands what a male doctor and female nurse duo did together with four hands. If it was a male doctor the accompanying midwife would hold the torch, or pass the equipment as required and reassure the patient. Even a few years later in the mid-1980s when I was a GP I'd be called out to catheterise male patients in their own homes as female district nurses were not allowed to touch men's penises – and they didn't stay to watch or help me either! But then when I was recently chatting to a nurse who works in an intensive care unit in the local hospital she said it's the same now – if a male patient needs catheterising, they call a male nurse to do it – even if he is working on a different ward!

You can look at this gender disharmony from the patient's perspective too. Pete still remembers when he was aged 22 years old in the early 1980s, feeling humiliated by a group of five female medical students aged about 19 years old grouping around the bottom of his theatre bed, and ogling him whilst he was being investigated for bleeding from his back passage. When he had a large metal pipe inserted up his anus to look for any cause of bleeding they took it in turns to peer in, with more or less body to body contact as he lay there semi-naked in a theatre gown with his bare bottom and trunk on display. He remembers thinking 'My God, make this end…..' This 'teaching' episode took place without Pete giving his consent as a patient, or being alerted before he climbed onto the bed that it was about to happen.

In the 1990s it was still the norm for male hospital consultants to be assertive, or even aggressive, with staff - just as they were in my junior doctor days in the 1970s. But when women doctors or nurses actually stood up to them, they were terrified that their seat on the throne was being threatened, and were really taken aback.

There was definite gender discrimination in nursing too, just as for doctors in those days. Male nurses rose up the career ladder much more quickly than female nurses did. It was assumed that male nurses would work full-time and female nurses only part-time so that they could tend to their family. Female nurses had to 'prove themselves' to get promotion at work.

In 1985 a friend of mine Dr Sharon started her first junior doctor post in surgery. As it happened, the other junior doctor covering a second surgical ward twinned with hers was a woman too. The ward sister was startled when they walked into together. She had never worked with any female doctor of any seniority on the surgery ward before – let alone get two of them at the same time! And with similar prejudice, women were still being discouraged from considering a surgical medical career in the 1990s; this can be seen by current NHS workforce statistics where a very small proportion of surgeons older than 50 years old are women, but there is more gender equity in younger consultant surgeons.

Dave who trained as a nurse in the late 1970s told me that one day in 1980 he was summoned by the hospital manager and told that he was moving him to take charge of an acute mental health ward in the hospital. He was to manage a ward with more than 26 patients as a newly qualified male nurse with help from one junior female nurse and a male auxiliary nurse who'd had elementary training. He did that for three years and was then moved on to take charge of an all female patient ward in the hospital and was the only member of staff who was a man – a real move towards gender equality in those days.

That level of sexism was rife in the attitude towards patients by doctors too. In the 1970s when Cath worked as a gynaecology nurse, she said that women who were booked in for a hysterectomy (having their womb surgically removed) for a medical reason, needed the consent of their husband if they were married. When Dr Fidelma became a consultant in that specialty in the 1990s there were very few women doctors working as consultants in hospital. Patients and staff regarded her as 'different' and thought she was 'snobby' as she was Irish with a strong accent. Many patients assumed that she was a nurse and not a doctor; just as they had regarded me as a junior doctor in hospitals in the early 1980s. Dr Fidelma learnt to stand up for herself, and still does!

I regarded being a general practitioner as an important career choice that I made, and I regarded doctors who were GPs or hospital consultants as equals. Being a GP then though was generally regarded as a career path for a doctor to fall back on, if they had not succeeded in progressing to becoming a hospital consultant in any medical specialty.

Of course, there may be a justified gender divide between doctors in the same medical specialty, or general practice in particular, if they are an expert in male or female health conditions. Some male GPs for instance, recognise that they are not fully competent in providing women's healthcare, especially as new treatments such as for the menopause evolve; and similarly, some women GPs might doubt their own competence about performing a prostate examination by sticking their fingers up a male patient's anus if they undertake such an examination very infrequently. The percentage of GPs who are female continues to climb – recent research has shown that female doctors derive more satisfaction than male doctors from their relationships with patients, are more likely to be working in training practices, but work fewer sessions per week. There is still a gender divide in the areas for which male and female GPs take lead responsibilities; with male doctors it's having a key interest in the practice computer system, doing minor surgery and overseeing the finances; whereas female GPs are not surprisingly more likely to look after women's healthcare.

I tried to develop a good work/life balance to make time for my family whilst starting and completing training to be a GP in the late 1970s; and then developing a portfolio career – with a mix of clinical practice and academia – much of which could be done by working from home for part of the time on evolving research papers and writing books. My husband gave up his job as a physiotherapist to look after our children after we both tried for a year working part-time, which we found difficult. If one of us ran late who'd look after our little kids when the other needed urgently to get to work? Having a stay at home dad gave us a settled family life so we started fostering too when our boys were aged 5 and 3 years old. It was very unusual in the 1980s though for a woman to work and have a house husband like I had.

My husband Chris went back to work as a part-time physio when our youngest kid went to school. Sometimes I had to step in with providing the child care – with my children coming along with me on home visits, staying in my car whilst I went into a patient's house; or sometimes they would sit in our general practice staff room doing jigsaws etc. I did prioritise my kids' preferences when I wanted to push on with my career progression. I wanted us to move to Warwick if I got to be a Professor of

General Practice in the newly growing University Medical School. I visited twice and met current staff and thought it very likely I'd be chosen as their Professor at a competitive interview. But discussing my hopes at home, it was clear that my teenage sons did NOT want to move 100 miles away and switch schools and would miss their friends – so I withdrew my application to the extreme annoyance of senior Medical School staff at Warwick University, with whom I'd met up as part of the application process.

A friend to whom I was chatting recently, described how she'd sacrificed her medical career to prioritise her husband's progression after completing her three year GP specialty training in the 1990s. She just took a one year temporary locum post and then had the first of her three children, following her husband around the country as his job locations changed. She had joined the GP retainer scheme when she was pregnant with her first child and stayed on doing two sessions per week in various general practices for many years – with maternity breaks. But she did not get any maternity pay for any of her three pregnancies/ postnatal terms as she had not been in the scheme long enough to qualify for pay linked to her first pregnancy, and then kept taking these unpaid breaks. Combining parenthood and a medical career is also a challenging issue faced by men nowadays. Alan, a core surgical trainee has had great difficulty getting agreement from the hospital management to reduce to a 60% time role, even though his educational supervisor had agreed that he could do so and just extend his surgery trainee programme for an extra year. He sought advice from the Local Medical Committee and its host, the British Medical Association (BMA) in their union role and succeeded in getting the hospital managers to agree to switch to his part-time working as a doctor, in his surgical role.

But the BMA hasn't always been so helpful in sorting gender discrimination. It went along with the gender inequalities relating to the spouse's share of a doctor's NHS pension if they died young in service, until 1989 and did not get a retrospective agreement in place. It was assumed before that, that the widow of a doctor who'd worked in the NHS needed and deserved 50% of their dead husband's pension following their death for as long as she lived. But it was not thought that a widower needed to access the pension of their dead medic wife because an adult man should be earning money from their own work, and not relying on their wife for a pensionable income after she died. If I'd died young whilst still practising as a doctor, my husband Chris, would only have got a 50% share of my pension for the years I'd worked from 1989 onwards and nil from the 15 years that I'd worked for the NHS before that time.

Historical workforce statistics show that in 1963 there were 22,159 GPs in England and Wales, 19,951 (90%) of whom were male and 2,208 (10%) of whom were female. Currently women make up about 58% of the general practitioner workforce, as a head count anyway – not necessarily as a percentage of the general practice work delivered, as female doctors are more likely to work part-time than their male GP colleagues.

There is still a sexist attitude now as to how banks/ mortgage/solicitors operate too; I heard from a friend recently that although she earns much more than her husband, the companies overseeing the purchase of her house and review of her mortgage all insisted on putting her husband Andy's name first, even though their mortgage was mainly based on her sizeable salary.

Chaperoning has always been an issue, and even nowadays there is quite a gender conundrum about arranging a chaperone, whilst a patient is having a hands on investigation of a private body part, like genitals, anus or breasts. As a female GP I would automatically ask my male patient if he would like a chaperone whilst I examined his prostate say, by putting my finger (in a sterile glove!!) up his anus. He'd typically check that this meant one of the nurses or health care assistants would be invited into join us, and when I'd confirm this, he'd decline the offer with something like 'Why would I want two women watching me - one is enough!' If I asked a female patient if she would like a chaperone before I performed a private examination, like examining her vagina or rectum, she'd usually decline too - relaying that she trusted me and didn't want another observer. The male GPs nearly always had a female chaperone join them when examining a female patient's breasts or other private area – they had to be pretty assertive about arranging this because they were far more likely to receive a complaint afterwards with the threat of litigation from a female patient who was displeased with them or distrustful, in some way. A few years ago, Dr Michael was suspended from medical practice for more than 18 months but was eventually found 'innocent' by a court. He hadn't asked his patient Sian if she wanted a chaperone to be present, because her sister was accompanying her already and was by her side in his consulting room. They made a complaint afterwards about his behaviour and so it was a battle for the truth, weighing both their statements against his – with no impartial chaperone present to give an independent view.

But it's not just patients who might be sexist. Abby who's currently a final year medical student told me that even trained female nurses on the hospital wards assume that she is a student nurse (she wears trousers, blouse, jacket and a lanyard on the wards) and not a medical student, although they recognise her male student friends as doctors-to-be, and not nurses. Even today on a staff ward round or an outpatient consultation in hospital, a patient can think that a male medical student is the doctor, and a more senior female hospital consultant, say on a gynaecology ward, is the nurse - just because of their gender. For some reason female doctors report too that they are expected to be nicer, tidier and more generous with their time, than male doctors are by their NHS managers. A recent survey by the BMA found that nine out of ten female doctors relayed that they had experienced sexism at work in the last two years; and 42% of doctors who had witnessed or experienced such sexism had not gone on to report it.

That gender bias is still rife in general practice settings too. Ian who's a practice manager in a deprived area can walk through the waiting room wearing a suit, and patients will often call out: 'Doctor, just whilst you're here…..'. So, sexism persists in the general population, especially amongst older patients.

And that brings me to one of my worst experiences of my life in relation to sexism and the belittling of my gender as a female doctor. Out of the blue, I was approached by the BBC to see if I would agree to being included in a Panorama programme to showcase how successful women doctors can be in their medical careers. Of course, things don't always go as well as you were expecting, and there can be set backs every so often. One of these for me was being tricked to appear on Panorama in 1997. I was too trusting. Until that time I'd always had good experiences with the media such as taking part in *Generations Talking,* a BBC documentary in 1980, when I was one of three doctors talking about changing times; or *Midlands Tonight* which was a BBC news programme in which I took part in 1995, where I was interviewed about doctors' stress levels and the GPs' support scheme I'd set up, whilst they followed me around on a typical working day in my practice; or BBC Pebble Mill in 1996 where I talked about the recruitment issues that were ongoing even then to get doctors working in general practice, and retain them there.

So, when a member of the BBC got in touch with me by phone in January 1997 and asked if I'd be willing to take part in a *Panorama* programme talking about how I'd developed a good balance as a woman between my successful career and my family life? I said 'yes'. Little did I know that they were out to shaft me with a hidden theme of how selfish some mums are, putting their careers before the needs of their children. They explained that there was only two weeks before the Panorama programme would be screened on TV, and we had to make arrangements for the two days that the Panorama film crew and team needed to spend with me, during the following week. I was promised that I could view the 20 minutes or so recording of the programme about me, before the day it was to be broadcast so that there was enough time to edit parts of the filming if I wanted any bits to be omitted. It was to be a one hour or so length programme with a few other women and their families included in different sections. Well!! This was a learning experience and I was far too trusting. I liked the two main producers when we met and spent two days together. One of the days I was at an important work meeting and was travelling by train from Stoke-on-Trent to London, leaving about 7am and returning about 8pm. The film crew and female producer followed me to London, had a break there and came back on the train with me again. They were aware that I usually went shopping in a main retail store on the way home to top up on food and household products for the family, and wanted me to do this. They even went to that retail store earlier that day to explain they'd be filming, and the manager got the staff all set up and ready (the Panorama crew did film me shopping there, but did not include those clips in the final version of the programme). Whilst I was away there was more filming at my home, egging on my oldest son Dave to cook for the family (food which my husband had prepared and would usually do). They interviewed our children individually – aged 12, 15 and 17 years old then – and tricked them into telling any personal stories about the hard lives they had with their mother away most days and how they had to cope by themselves somehow. It was all nonsense as my husband Chris just worked for three mornings per week as a part-time physiotherapist so he was always able to take and fetch the children to and from school, run them to after school clubs or to their piano lessons or other commitments. As a full-time academic doctor and sessional GP in 1997, I worked from home on my research and writing much of the time. We were a really happy and thriving family, but the Panorama remit was to show what a dreadful state of affairs it was if a mum had a career and worked full-time. They treated the other three women appearing on this Panorama programme in the same way. The aim of the programme for all of us seemed to be to humiliate us as selfish working mums and they called the episode, *Missing Mum*. One of the producers was a working mum herself with a one year old child whom she'd left with her own mother to look after whilst she was away for two days, as she lived in London, and had to stay overnight in a hotel in Stoke-on-Trent to do the two days of my filming. She was the one who interviewed each of my kids whilst they were being filmed and pushed them into each relaying untrue scenarios – what a fraud she was! After the show anyone who knew me was so angry that Panorama had portrayed me as a selfish, soul-less mum. Our children's piano teacher was so shocked at how we'd been represented as work-centric parents in the programme which she knew first hand was not true, and wanted to start a campaign to protest about Panorama's despicable behaviour.

Having represented the purpose of the programme to be a spotlight on how parents were managing roles in a changing society, it was only mentioned by the producer on the last day of filming that some un-reviewed research had shown that the male children of working mothers did less well at school. It then became clear that their disturbing pursuit of our 15-year-old son, manipulating him into making statements which he instantly regretted, was part of a different agenda. So, too, was the focus on the cooking skills of our older son, rather than his academic achievements (he eventually gained a PhD in chemistry at Oxford before completing a medical degree). We were mere pawns in a story created by Panorama, to support a rather weak research paper.

The programme was a topic of discussion on Any Questions that week, and Chris phoned in to the Any Answers programme to explain how we had been duped into being actors in a Panorama drama, rather than it being a true documentary. (This was at a time when Panorama was regarded by many as an unbiased news programme; it was before the advent of 'reality TV'.) As a consequence of Chris's intervention, he was invited to participate in a Biteback programme, which provided an opportunity for participants to question the integrity of the Panorama programme makers. Although the producer had misled us, and made promises which were never kept (such as our opportunity to veto material before transmission) the BBC response was still to deny any failure to follow procedures.

On reviewing the programme with the benefit of hindsight, it is clear that the ethos of Panorama had changed from the trustworthy documentary maker of previous decades to be a programme designed to capture public interest, no matter who was harmed in the process, rather like a tabloid newspaper might do. A preceding programme was called 'Dumping Granny' where a hapless couple were portrayed as heartlessly walking away from their responsibilities, when the facts were apparently more nuanced than represented on TV, and which left the pair alienated in their community. Of course, this was just over a year later than the Panorama programme where Princess Diana was duped to describe on air all manner of thoughts which might have been better left unsaid. By comparison, the outrage experienced by our family was insignificant.

When I was in Edinburgh airport a couple of weeks later waiting in the departure lounge for my flight back to Manchester after the one-day conference I'd presented at, a total stranger came up to me. "It was you on Panorama last week, wasn't it? I thought how they treated you was absolutely dreadful – I don't know how they could treat your family like that." I declined her offer to make a complaint, but I really appreciated that another working mum whom I'd never met felt so strongly about the barbaric twisted pitch of the Panorama team - just to get their audience spellbound - never mind if it was a bunch of lies. I had a similar expression of support from a conductor on the Manchester/London trainline; if he was on duty when I was travelling to work by train over the next few years, he'd invite me to move free of charge from second class to the first class train carriage, or slip me a free cup of coffee – or even wine; this was to put out a friendly arm of support and sympathy for me – not trying to get to know a famous Panorama star better!

After that I signed up for media training and became a lot more media savvy; and focused on my writing on the whole, rather than any more TV appearances! I certainly felt sympathy for Princess Diana as to how Panorama treated her a year or so earlier by misrepresenting her passion and achievements in her royal and family lives. I relate to that even now, especially as the daily newspapers are still updating us about the ongoing Freedom of Information requests relating to how BBC chiefs were involved and whether they had withheld information about how Martin Bashir had clinched his interview with Princess Diana on Panorama in 1995.

To overcome stereotyping as I've aged, I've continued to dye my hair to fit in better alongside my younger colleagues. I tend to wear red or bright coloured clothes if I'm talking at a conference or attending an important NHS meeting. I purposely choose to wear modern vintage type jackets to fit in with others. I learnt to look fairly inconsequential and part of the 'wallpaper' early on in my medical career, then step forward and interact if I want to get attention and make a point, with a worthwhile purpose.

Racism seems to be in parallel with sexism and ageism, in the main. Three fifths of international medical graduates who are practising doctors in the UK recently reported that they often experience racism when working in the NHS – from patients and other members of staff. I heard about a medical student with Afro hair being forced to wear two hair nets tied together as no big hair nets were available and the theatre nurse insisted that every strand of her hair must be within the net or she must step outside – even though the student was just observing surgery, not doing it. That really upset her.

Recently a hospital consultant asked a medical student with dark skin to talk to a patient who couldn't speak English. He assumed that just because they had dark skin they could speak any African/Asian language. Of course, they couldn't – the patient who was from the Congo had a very specific dialect and the medical student came from India originally. She's also only just about five feet tall and she's been told several times that she's not old enough to be a medical student and is a child (though she's actually aged 22 years old)!

And how is it now?

So how do we reduce sexism in healthcare? A recent survey found that 91% of female doctors reported experiencing sexism at work in the last three or so years. And an NHS national staff survey in 2020 found that over 20% staff cited their gender, leading to discrimination at work.

There is still a gender split these days in choice of medical specialty, or rather which medical specialties, female doctors are welcomed to join. There are still very few female surgeons for instance (16%), whilst the majority of doctors working in obstetrics and gynaecology are female (61%). The medical student intake these days is disproportionally female (62%) with as many as 72% being female, in Northern Ireland medical schools.

This gender pay gap still features in the medical workforce, partly reflecting the different roles that women opt for. For example, in general practice there seems to be a gender pay gap of about 34%, as fewer female GPs opt for partnerships and may prefer salaried or locum roles, or choose to work fewer hours per week.

But it's not just the NHS where there is not a fair gender ethos. One rail company highlighted recently that it hopes that in future at least one-fifth of new trainee drivers will be women, with a target of achieving an equal gender split for new recruits by 2030. Only 13 per cent of its total driver workforce are female at present.

Proposals to amend UK legislation to describe the menopause as a 'protected characteristic' under the Equality Act were recently rejected by the UK government due to fears that it could discriminate against men if there were 'unintended consequences ……. for example, discrimination risks towards men suffering long-term medical conditions'.

In the general population, women in England typically earn a quarter less income than men from their work, pensions and investments. Male taxpayers are reported to have earned an average £42,000 in a recent tax year, whilst women had an average income of £31,100, according to a recent report published by HM Revenue and Customs. Women are more likely to take on caring responsibilities, which can hinder their career progression as well as their capacity to work full-time. This income gap is reportedly at its widest when men and women are in their fifties, when women generally have an average income around a third less than men's. On the other hand, there's a national disparity between statutory maternity and statutory paternity pay, where new fathers who are employed in work are only entitled to two weeks, and new mothers are able to take 52 weeks' leave from work, 39 of which are paid – though not fully.

Chapter 4. How stressful is working in the NHS?

What is work based stress?

Stress is an abnormal response to pressure and tension. Almost everyone experiences it. In small doses over short periods of time it can help to boost someone's performance. Problems arise though when stress levels become too high and last too long. So, there is a continuum ranging from the stress you'd expect to experience as short-lived unease or mild tension, to extreme stress or distress where you'd feel panic, fear or terror.

Stress is a sort of balance between the demands you're experiencing, your feelings about those demands and your ability to cope with them. Work stress is common when your workload is high, control over your workload is limited, and there is too little support or help available for you. That can affect your performance too – if your concentration gets worse, you're more irritable and get further and further behind with your workload, and then feel more and more guilt and shame and worry about missing timelines and the lower standards of your work. You might become more withdrawn, tearful, sensitive, agitated or aggressive. The more stressed you become, the harder it is to stay on top of your work, especially if you are experiencing guilt or shame, creating a vicious circle of stress which feeds on itself- one factor can make the next stage worse.

Common stressors for those working within the NHS are relationship clashes between staff and their managers, making mistakes, conflicting priorities with progressing their career and family life, fear of litigation, and the very many demands from their work, that can overload them. An over-stressed doctor or nurse may become withdrawn and uncommunicative at home after dealing with demanding patients or managers, so that their personal relationships may then become more strained, especially if they have to juggle their hours of work with parental or caring responsibilities. Providing childcare is consistently raised as a challenge by parents working in the NHS, whose rotas or daily roles often include long and unpredictable working days so that childcare does not fit easily with their working patterns. A recent survey of NHS staff described as many as two-thirds of survey respondents expressing regret for the family sacrifices that they have made over the years for the sake of their clinical careers. I can't say that applies to me – I'm proud of how my husband and I each worked out our work/family life balance so that he became the house daddy for eight or so years working at most three sessions a week as a physiotherapist, supporting me as a full-time GP. And then I was working more flexibly for the subsequent ten or so years as an academic with just one or two sessions a week as a GP, whilst our three children grew up to be more self-sufficient.

Work stress can be contagious, having knock on effects on those around you. Staff may feel like 'piggies in the middle' between their NHS employers and their patients. If a receptionist books extra patients in to a half-day clinic because there is such high patient need, the doctors may yell at them, as it puts such additional person strain upon them. But if they do not accommodate those patients in need of medical appointments, the receptionists may incur the patients' wrath instead.

Sometimes it is being in dangerous situations like the fear of being assaulted by a patient or actually having been attacked, that can trigger real pressure, especially if a doctor or nurse is doing a home visit on their own. I will always remember being called out to assess John, a 45 year old patient, in my first few years as a GP. He'd requested the visit because he had muscle pains and was feeling low and didn't feel able to walk to the surgery for a consultation. I sat down on a chair in John's lounge opposite where he was sitting to start a friendly doctor/patient chat, when I was suddenly aware that he had placed a dangerous looking large knife on the table sited between us, pointed at me. I then had to dredge up all my 'kind doctor' talking skills, which resulted in him getting up to go and fetch something from another room; I then stood up too and walked into the hall to stand at the front door and conclude our medical review.

After that experience I always made sure on a home visit that I was the one near the exit door, and the patient walked into their lounge or kitchen in front of me for our consultation. On other occasions when I anticipated I might be exposed to a personal risk I would leave my mobile phone on whilst in the patient's house with a staff member listening if in the daytime, or my husband if I was doing a home visit after hours, if I thought that there was any chance that I was about to visit a 'mad' patient. By being proactive I felt in control, and avoided feeling stressed by this potentially dangerous aspect of my medical work. You can even feel at risk from a patient becoming violent when sitting at your desk in a clinic consultation room during the daytime – then you hope that by pressing the panic button (if you've got one to hand) you will alert work colleagues that you've a patient becoming violent or threatening, and they can come along immediately to step in to help. These days the practice computer will have a panic button that a staff member can press readily – as opposed to the old days when the panic device might have been stored in a drawer and not readily available, or the battery might have needed replacing!

It wasn't just potential danger that triggered work stress for me undertaking home visits as a GP though. Sometimes it was being unexpectedly called upon to undertake a medical task beyond my competency. In the 1980s, a patient would call their GP for an emergency home visit, whereas now it would be a 999 call for an ambulance or contacting 111 for advice on whether to get straight to the accident and emergency department – or what? One day at 2pm on a sunny afternoon when I was in the middle of my GP clinic, there was a phone call to the practice receptionist requesting a home visit to see Anna, a 19 year old girl who was moaning about her tummy pain. Reception put the call through for me to judge how urgent it was as I was the GP covering all emergencies for that day, as well as handling my booked eight patients per hour for the three hours afternoon session. I just had an inkling that I should hurry over to see the girl and apologised to those patients who were already sitting in the waiting room that there might be an extra 30 minutes or so delay in them being seen. Our GP surgery was sited in a small town but Anna lived out in the sticks in a rural setting about five miles away. When I arrived and got out of my car, her mother shouted out to me in a frantic state and rushed me to the bathroom – for there was Anna crouching over the toilet with a baby hanging out still attached by its umbilical cord with its head just above the water. So, I grabbed and supported the baby whilst her mum helped Anna up and we walked her to the nearby couch in their sitting room. I asked her mum to call an ambulance and explain the emergency. It was about six years since I'd delivered a baby as part of my junior doctor training, but I knew to physically support Anna's newborn baby and keep it warm lying on Anna's tummy, and not to try and cut off the umbilical cord without any equipment. I kept up the 'confident' doctor act until the ambulance team turned up 20 minutes or so later and they took over lifting Anna and her baby into their ambulance and caring for her, with help from a midwife they'd picked up on the way. And Anna really hadn't known she was pregnant until her baby popped out when she was sitting on that toilet with such tummy pains!

Then of course I had to dash back to my GP surgery and work through the backlog of patients who'd been waiting for more an hour for their booked GP appointments, focussing on each individual patient and their concerns and not letting the exciting newborn baby delivery intrude into my thoughts. When I was telling a consultant obstetrician this patient story recently, Dr Fidelma shared that she still sees about six women a year even these days, who do not know that they are pregnant – and they can be 34, or 36 or even 40 weeks pregnant and still be unaware. She has seen a few who were unaware they were pregnant and went into labour, just as for my experience with Anna. These women are usually obese and thus their stomach bulging from being too fat has disguised their pregnancy from the mum-to-be, her partner and others close to her.

When I visited Anna at home a week or so later for a follow-up home visit, she had adjusted well to motherhood as had the new grandparents. I had had to deal with a very stressful situation, but with such a successful outcome my experience of that medical emergency visit turned into a positive one, rather than my being riddled with fear and 'what ifs?'. Doctors survive by being resilient and not overly emotional; they should be good timekeepers but need to be flexible if an essential patient consultation needs more justifiable time than was expected or booked.

From personal stories I've read over the decades, doctors are very vulnerable to patient complaints which are really related to personal gripes, rather than substantial professional wrong-doing, and these trigger lots of episodes of personal stress. I experienced such a complaint in the 1980s when I was a full-time GP partner. It was merely that a woman who'd come to see me with discomfort of her abdomen wanted to claim the money back she lost when two weeks later she could not go on a pre-booked holiday because she was having an operation on her womb.

When she initially came to see me it sounded as if she had a possible irritable bowel from the way she described her mild symptoms and I examined her stomach as she lay on the bed in my consulting room, and I then prescribed her treatment accordingly. At a follow-up appointment two weeks later her abdominal pains were worsening and now she had some unexplained bleeding and so I undertook an internal examination where I wondered if she had some abnormality and referred her to a hospital specialist, who when he saw her two weeks later wanted to operate and advised her to delay her holiday.

My medical defence organisation chose to settle out of court as it was cheaper for them to reimburse some of her holiday costs, than pay for their lawyers to defend me. That was very annoying as however many times I re-assessed the medical care I'd provided for her, the more convinced I was that I'd acted correctly as her doctor. If I was to have undertaken internal medical examinations of women every time they described some vague tummy aches, then I'd have got many more patients' complaints about my being intrusive and over-zealous. That's actually the only time in my medical career of 40 plus years of frontline practice that I've had a patient complaint that's involved my medical indemnity organisation.

I've just read of a similar story from a well known doctor who writes in medical newspapers, where her indemnity organisation settled out of court too, just to draw the patient complaint to a close, rather than investigate the truth – I was not surprised to read that she felt crushed by them rewarding the patient as I had done, rather than rejecting the unfounded complaint.

I did work at a national level in the mid-1990s to create a national model for occupational health services support for GPs; it partly worked out with the pilot we set up in Staffordshire and local healthcare organisations generally making it possible for staff in self-employed healthcare settings like general practices to be referred to occupational health services elsewhere, mirroring that available for those working in hospital and community healthcare settings. These days there are wellbeing support services available to all doctors and medical students, plus their partners and dependents, that is run by the British Medical Association which is confidential and free of charge, and very well thought of. There's other support available to healthcare workers in the UK too, such as staff mental health and wellbeing hubs, workforce specialty services, employee assistance programmes and NHS helplines.

And now

Sickness absence amongst NHS staff is still a problem. Statistics collected in 2023 gave an overall sickness rate for NHS staff in England as 5.0%, and the rate in 2024 seems a bit lower still at 4.7%. The highest sickness rates in staff groups in March 2024 for example were those working for Ambulance Trusts (6.5%); and the lowest rate of 3.2% were for management staff working for Integrated Care Boards. Around a quarter of sick days are blamed on anxiety, stress, depression and other psychiatric ill-health. Not surprising then that work stress and burnout are often cited as reasons why NHS staff decide to retire early; so, in the year between September 2022 to 2023, about 20,000 doctors are estimated to have quit working in the NHS, ahead of their retirement age.

Chronic excessive workload is one of the most important causes of work-related stress, and yet it is increasingly normalised for NHS staff to have multiple competing, urgent pressures, and for these to overlap with making major clinical decisions. In a recent national NHS staff survey, 45% of staff reported feeling unwell because of work-related stress, and only half thought that they had a good work-life balance. Those most likely to report work-related stress were paramedics (64%) and midwives (63%). The impact of work stress was also captured by a survey of GPs across the UK soon after which noted that '23% of GPs across the UK were so stressed that they felt they couldn't cope many days or every day' and nearly all of the GPs responding (84%) reported working way more than their contracted hours on most days. Three quarters of nurses from all NHS settings described how they regularly worked beyond their contracted hours too at least once per week, with many of these hours being unpaid. Of course, this generates increasing numbers of doctors and nurses leaving work because they are exhausted or burnt out. Then the increasing vacancy rates in the NHS put more demand on those left behind practising healthcare.

Many doctors and nurses describing their work-related stress term it as 'burnout', meaning that it is a chronic problem and not just confined to a day or two here and there, which generates feelings of exhaustion, negative or cynical attitudes to work, and sometimes poor professional performance. As many as 49% of ambulance staff reported feeling burnt out in another recent national survey, compared with 40% of registered nurses and midwives, and 35% of hospital-based medical and dental staff. Recent research by the General Medical Council (GMC) reported that nearly a quarter of doctors (23%) had taken leave of absence due to stress in the previous year; 28% of doctors working in hospitals and 43% of GPs indicated that burnout and work-related stress were the prime reasons that they had been absent from work. A recent workforce census found that two out of five hospital consultants report having an excessive workload, and two-thirds were somewhat, or very, stressed at work. In another recent survey, GPs were almost twice as likely to describe experiencing burnout (43%) compared to hospital-based specialist doctors (22%). And these aren't just words and political descriptions. I'm describing real people here – like Gail who committed suicide recently; her husband blamed her long-standing intolerable nurse workload as the main factor in Gail taking her own life that pushed her to the brink. Another recent national survey found that poor mental health accounted for almost a quarter of sick days taken by staff working in hospital and community health settings, which included anxiety, stress, depression and other psychiatric illnesses.

Several years on after the COVID calamity, doctors' experiences of stress are even worse than they've ever been, according to a recent survey of 4,000 doctors from all types of clinical workplaces. Nearly half of the doctors surveyed described their struggles to provide 'sufficient patient care' (inadequate staffing levels were a common reason for this) and a quarter were deemed to be at high risk of burnout; most reported working far more hours than they were contracted for, each week, and this was becoming more and more frequent, with much less opportunity for rest breaks too when at work. The good news was though that around half of the doctors surveyed still reported feeling satisfied in their workplace – in a hospital, community care or general practice.

A main stressor that GPs and their practice teams often describe as inducing their work-stress is the setting of national targets each year for them to attain in the delivery of their practice care which is not necessarily patient-centred; failure to meet these targets will damage their annual income that they need to survive as small businesses. The preparation needed to get ready for external quality visits and inspections by organisations such as the Care Quality Commission takes its toll too on everyone involved in the practice – clinicians, the manager and the administrative team.

Racism can be another factor in generating work stress. A recent annual report published by the GMC described how about twice as many doctors from ethnic minority groups compared to 'white' doctors were referred to the GMC following fitness to practise complaints from their employers. They concluded that there is a need for a 'supportive and inclusive' ethos in NHS settings and condemned racism towards staff in any healthcare settings. Another recent national racism in medicine survey relayed that two in five doctors reported experiencing derogatory comments from patients about their ethnicity, country of origin, heritage, name or accent. The British Medical Association (BMA) – their so called 'doctors' union' – relayed that 9% of doctors responding to their recent annual survey reported that they had left their jobs because of experiencing racism in their workplace. And those who are part of the LGBTQ+ community described taking sick leave or time off due to the discrimination that they experienced too.

A recent review by the General Medical Council, found that doctors are often taking preventive action to protect themselves from burnout; by reducing their working hours, refusing additional work, and even considering leaving the NHS, or giving their notice in as they cannot cope with their extensive working hours. So many of those surveyed described working beyond their rostered hours on a regular basis, and being forced to change their working practices to sustain their own wellbeing and their patients' safety. Doctors with disabilities were very likely to describe how they were struggling with their workload and feared that the care they were providing to patients was not good enough. And doctors working in general practice were much more likely than doctors in other medical specialties to report these work stress pressures. Some recent research has shown that mental distress is high amongst doctors working in many different countries. There are comparatively high rates of suicide among female doctors, which are often put down to contributing factors such as discrimination and sexual harassment, as well as hefty working hours that prevent the affected doctor from having a sensible work-life balance.

Some doctors recognise the effects of work stress upon them and make career changing decisions to cut down their working hours and/or reduce their responsibilities. Dr Mark for instance, used to work around 60 hours a week as a norm as a GP partner in a deprived area, as well as being a prison doctor and a clinical director with a mental health trust. Now recognising the toll that the demands of these three clinical roles were taking on him, he has cut down to less than 50 hours a week focussed on his GP role as a partner with three regular days in practice (10 hour days if he's lucky) and working alongside as a GP locum or for the 'Out of Hours' service with the additional working hours of his choosing that allow him to adopt a healthy lifestyle and prioritise some family time.

Work stress is wide-ranging and endemic in the health service. It includes real challenges from all sorts of factors in the NHS such as (mis)organisation, personal stresses, time pressures, relationship stresses (at work or home, between clinicians/managers or colleagues), professional regulatory stresses, rota stresses and interface stresses between teams and different health and care sectors, as well as the common understaffing of all types of clinicians of all levels of seniority. The NHS needs to address all of these stressors proactively and urgently to retain its workforce and sustain the health service at scale.

If it doesn't, yet more NHS staff will be resigning from their posts and seeking new jobs overseas. The NHS has apparently become a net exporter of doctors these days, with one in seven UK based doctors who've recently trained now working overseas. Work stress and burnout are often cited as reasons for doctors to quit the UK and transfer to working abroad in sunnier climes with higher rates of pay and hoped for better working conditions. Though of course, we still import lots of doctors and nurses too, who come to work in our NHS from other countries abroad who can't afford to lose their trained clinicians either.

Sometimes qualified nurses who come to work in the UK believing there are great career opportunities here are taken aback to find out that they need to pass an English language qualification to be a registered NHS professional, and if their English language skills are not good enough, they end up working as health care assistants on much lower pay grades, until they have improved and passed the language test – if they ever do! Requalifying to work as a registered nurse in the UK is a considerable source of work and personal stress for them.

Chapter 5. Asylum, or so called sanctuary

The group of Mary Dendy Homes for the 'mentally subnormal' based in Cheshire was founded in 1908, then joined the NHS as the Mary Dendy Hospital in 1948. This mental hospital was out in the wilds away from the town centre and was known locally as a 'lunatic asylum'. It continued to accommodate as many as 375 mentally handicapped people until it closed in 1986. In 1982 when I took on my first salaried GP post with rural GP Dr D, I was employed by Macclesfield District Health Authority to provide general practice related care for three half-day sessions a week. In addition, Dr D or I could be called out night or day to provide urgent medical help that the hospital psychiatrists did not feel was in their remit. I would review wards of inmates and individual patients whom the nurses picked out for each of my half-day sessions. Many women had resided there for decades – some had been first admitted as a teenager for having an illegitimate baby (even if that was as a result of rape). The baby would have been taken off them for adoption without their informed consent. They'd been holed up there ever since, confined in the hospital without their agreement. Post-natal depression was another common reason for a woman to have been admitted to such an asylum, over the decades.

By 1890, over 60 asylums were built and opened in England, and had become virtually self-sufficient communities. Most were built on the edge of towns with living quarters, chapels, farms, gardens and workshops to encourage employment. Women inmates might do sewing or laundry or general housekeeping duties around the ward. The mantra was that the justification for the incarceration of many of these patients was that they were being protected from the stresses of the outside world, whilst receiving treatment for their mental health conditions.

Staffordshire's three asylums were purpose-built, aiming to provide therapeutic, yet secure, settings. A superintendent was in charge of an asylum with assistant medical officers. A matron managed the female staff and patients. Day-to-day patient care was overseen by the keepers who often had minimal education. Female staff were required to leave their employment at an asylum when they married.

The use of mechanical restraint was common until the late 1830s, justified as preventing violent patients from injuring themselves or others, self-harming, or being aggressive towards others. The most common restraints were the straight jacket and fingerless gloves. As time went on, patients were encouraged to take on work, or exercise in the open air, diverting them from having irrational thoughts and their personal preoccupations.

In the early 20th century male and female patients were allowed to mix during the day but slept in same sex wards, which might be locked to keep inmates secure. Wards were able to house up to 50 patients, in close proximity, with little personal space - and privacy was minimal. Sick and infirm patients stayed in their own dedicated wards and spent the majority of their time shut in there. Angry, violent or suicidal patients were sometimes housed in padded cells. In some asylums, patients might be regularly dosed with paraldehyde in the evenings to calm them down and ease the staff workload.

In the 1930s, two major treatments took centre stage for severe mental health problems. These were electroconvulsive therapy (ECT) delivered by passing an electrical current through the brain, and lobotomy. Lobotomy involved cutting out the brain tissue within the frontal lobes of the brain; this had mixed results and so was discontinued in the 1950s. ECT was effective for patients suffering from severe depression and is still very occasionally used today. I witnessed its use in person on a patient of mine in the mid-1990s, triggering epileptic fits in the midst of the procedure. Yes, it helped with his depression when a range of prescribed drugs had had little effect, but it wiped out a good deal of his memories of holidays and family time - a hard price to pay.

In 1948, Section 47 of the newly agreed National Assistance Act enabled the compulsory detention of a person (described as being 'sectioned') where it was in their best interests, or would prevent them from injuring other people. Two registered doctors were required to independently certify that their detention was justified. Alcoholism, and the associated delusion, were common reasons for such certification.

The traditional asylum gradually had fewer long-term patients to care for as new psychiatric treatments and medication were more effective, and patients with mental health disorders could be kept at home or receive community care. In-patient numbers reduced from over 150,000 in mental hospitals in England in 1950 to 80,000 in 1975. With the passing of the Mental Health Act in 1983, people committed to asylums were given back their full rights and could appeal their certification. However, some individuals still seemed to miss out on getting a fair hearing – a mental health nurse told me the other day about George's life story.
He was admitted to an asylum in the 1970s, aged 14 years old. He had a mental health problem described as attention deficit disorder and was seen by a local person to be urinating in a park, in a bush. His action was interpreted incorrectly by others as masturbating and reported to the police – with the implication that he was a child sexual predator. This was then entered on his medical records without any police investigation or official confirmation. George always denied it. His parents agreed that he should be admitted to a mental asylum as he was such a difficult teenager; he was never released nor investigated. More than 43 years later when he was 57 years old, George was still being held in a secure unit in a private mental health hospital; he was described in his medical records as a 'sexual deviant' even though there had never been any explicit proof of such a disorder, and he'd been 'locked up' ever since without him having any say in his continuing detention.

The Cheddleton mental asylum in Staffordshire, was set up in 1899 and morphed into St Edward's Hospital with the creation of the NHS in 1948. St Edward's was closed in 2002 and redeveloped to provide residential housing. This was the third County asylum to be established in Staffordshire, as in the 1890s the other two were so overcrowded. It had 16 wards for up to 618 patients. It was soon extended to provide accommodation for 1038 patients with similar numbers of male and female patients. I recently visited a touring exhibition capturing the history of this asylum and learnt about a woman who had spent 70 years there after she was wrongly accused of theft. Joan now 85 years old, was working as a cleaner in a doctor's surgery when she was accused of stealing 2s 6d. The cash later turned up but by then Joan had been sectioned. Her two much younger brothers found out that the sister they had thought was dead decades before, was still alive and living in care.

Her brother, now 63 years old, reported that: "Last month I received a questionnaire from a care home in Macclesfield. It was addressed to my mother and I was just about to throw it in the bin as junk when I saw a name that I recognised pencilled in the corner. I rang them and they said straight away that our sister was living there." Earlier this year the brothers made their first visit to see Joan at the care home and said: "It's been emotional. Nowadays there are reviews and appeals but back then, a doctor could sign away a person's life with the stroke of a pen- it's a terrible waste." But this unfair incarceration of Joan in an asylum, and then being transferred on to a mental hospital was not unusual.

A nurse with whom I met up recently remembers caring for so many women patients in their 50s and 60s in the 1970s when she was doing her nurse training, who'd been admitted to an asylum when they had had an illegitimate pregnancy, decades before. Cath recalls a lady aged 35 years old visiting one of the residents fifteen years older than her who was her birth mother, and still a resident in the mental hospital for no other reason than she had had an illegitimate child and had then become institutionalised, and unable to be discharged to live an independent life.

Another example of injustice that's come to light from my chatting to people, is from the 1970s in Hereford where a local asylum called 'The Haven' was known to be full of 'naughty girls'. Many of these were young mums who had had illegitimate children. They were admitted when they were pregnant and they stayed until the children were aged 2-3 years old and were then moved on. They were often seen as an outcast by their family – to be hidden away. Some were moved on to a community base in Shrewsbury, 60 miles away, which was very disruptive to them in trying to regain a normal life, and where their location was outside of their control.

A common approach for parents to take in the 1970s, when a girl like Sheila became pregnant at the age of 15 years old, was to send their teenage daughter away to stay with a distant family member; for Sheila this was Northern Ireland when she was three months pregnant. Once she'd given birth, she and baby Fiona returned to her family where the new baby was brought up by Sheila's mother, (really grandma Ellen) as her own child. Ellen had been pretending to neighbours and friends in the few months before Sheila and her baby returned home that she was pregnant. So, no one suspected – even Sheila's young sister Kellie who was aged six years old at the time, didn't know that Fiona was her niece and not her younger sister, until she was in her thirties when it all came out at Ellen's funeral!

Mental health nurse Dave, was telling me how he'd worked as a nursing cadet at St Edward's mental hospital in the early 1970s, starting at the age of 16 years old. He then progressed to do his mental health nurse training at St Edward's in 1975-1978. In those days nurses were not trained at a university but were taught in classrooms in the hospital, with lots of hands on training on different hospital wards as 'free labour'. Once trained, nurse Dave managed 69 deranged, chronically mentally ill patients squashed in an all male ward, designed for a maximum of 50 patients. They had no personal belongings, no privacy, and shared communal clothing – all supplied by the hospital. There was a 'First up, best dressed' patient mantra. Dave was the charge nurse with one auxiliary nurse and a ward orderly, doing 13 hours shifts for three and a half days each week (so, that's a minimum of 46 paid hours each week). He then handed over nursing responsibilities for the next 12 hours overnight to only one person. So, he did plenty of overtime. He was appalled at the setting that these 69 male patients were being kept in, confined in the ward all day. He used his initiative and the hospital boss agreed, to get patients more active by organising walks for groups of patients outside, every day. He was warned by other ward managers that he was taking risks doing this, but he was driven to provide better care for the men whom he looked after. At the time very many of his patients were heavily dependent on prescribed drugs like phenothiazines. I heard that there were some repercussions though at St Edwards from letting these patients out for exercise. One patient Sam, was obsessed with nicking petrol caps from cars parked in the hospital grounds. Mental health nurse Maggie tried to stop him and the patient punched Maggie in the face; seeing this, a male nurse stepped in and grabbed Sam and hit him..and kept on hitting and kicking him to punish him for pinching those petrol caps, so he wouldn't do it again. As a result of this, Sam had to be taken to the local Accident and Emergency department with blood streaming from his nose after the aggressive behaviour of the male nurse (against whom no action was taken by the hospital manager or matron).

But the regular exercise that Dave had initiated continued and once it was obvious that the ward inmates were happier out walking than when they'd been confined to their ward all day, other ward managers started to copy the approach and regular daily exercise became the norm.

As Dave progressed in mental health nursing he was brought in to aid an external enquiry at St Edwards– which resulted in 77 recommendations. From that, he was parachuted in as an emergency as Director of Nursing - a real accolade. The hospital was £500,000 overspent (which was a lot of money in those days, in the 1980s). The other senior staff were pretty hostile, as every week their attempted progress to act on the myriad of recommendations was challenged by the external health authority team. But the quality of care improved immensely across the hospital. At least the care that the patients experienced in St Edward's asylum though was not as bad as what Dave witnessed when he joined a quality improvement team invited to Russia (Moscow & Stalingrad), in the early 1990s. He had full access to all their mental hospitals where cages in the wards for restraining patients were the norm and frequently used. Haloperidol was the drug commonly used there to sedate patients. Dave taught the Russian mental health teams about 'reasonable restraint' for their inmates, helping them to learn how they could provide much more patient-centred psychiatric services and adopt a 'whole person' approach that considered people's physical health, as well as their mental health and wellbeing. He helped senior people in Russia to create outreach polyclinics in the community to support patients who were discharged from hospital and keep them safely at home. He then repeated this advisory review on the quality and scope of mental health care services in Northern Croatia, in the late 1990s.

The Mental Health Act in 1983, aimed to provide safeguards against abuse generated by compulsory hospital admission. A patient could be detained for up to 28 days initially if they were suffering from a mental disorder which warranted assessment, or if they were a danger to themselves or others. The application for this assessment had to be made by a social worker or near relative, with a medical recommendation by two practising doctors of which one must specialise in psychiatry and the other know the patient well. Once the section was approved, the patient could be detained in a mental health facility for up to six months.

Whilst Kevin was working at the local 'insane' asylum (as he called it) during his adult nurse training in the mid-1980s, he thought that most of the regular nursing staff were not quite right in the head, in a number of ways! They seemed to be suffering from mental health problems too, so it seemed a strange place to work for his two months placement. Even though he was only a student nurse they were happy for Kevin to deliver whatever patient care he wanted, without formal supervision. Many of the patients had been there for very many years with various psychiatric conditions and had had burr holes drilled into their skulls in a misguided attempt to cure them, by releasing pressure on their brains. It seemed like medieval torture to Kevin. To reduce the effects of institutionalisation, the hospital ward manager had decided that the charge nurse would no longer control the patients' cigarettes. Up until this point each patient had their own pocket money to spend each week, and every one of the 30 male patients on the ward smoked like it was going out of style. Each patient spent their weekly allowance on about 40 cigarettes a day. The charge nurse would usually spend most of his shift as the tobacco controller. This meant that he had a stream of smokers knocking on his office door all day long for him to issue one cigarette at a time. As soon as they had smoked that cigarette they'd go back and ask for another. The biggest and strongest nurses and orderlies would carry a 'crash' bleep to indicate if one of the patients had kicked off and urgent assistance was required. On the day of the new system all the patients were given their day's allowance of cigarettes first thing in the morning. Most of them were capable of understanding that they had to ration them out to make them last all day. Understanding however is not the same as having the will power to do so. When the first patient, Neville, had finished all his fags the charge nurse told Kevin: 'Just wait now, it won't be long before they kick off', and how right he was. The charge nurse pulled the emergency bell which triggered the crash bleep. They managed to intervene in the fighting as about six staff tried to restrain Neville. They had him pinned down on the floor but he was throwing the staff around like rag dolls. Then he started to urinate, with everybody sliding about and falling over and getting thoroughly covered in wee!

Nurse Ann still remembers the very many doses of paraldehyde she drew up at the start of each of her shifts when she was working in an asylum in the 1970s. These were drawn up in glass syringes as a routine at the start of each shift, ready for when the patients were kicking off, for them to be given as a hypnotic sedative; the drug was regarded as being 'special' and couldn't be drawn up in the usual plastic syringes. These days a nurse would need a prescribing qualification to be able to draw up such a drug, initiate it and stab the patient with the needle!

When Ann did her nurse training in the early 1970s, there were lots of young children living in the Stallington mental health hospital too. Many of these young children were disabled. Ann remembers one little boy, Stuart, who had devastating brain damage after being beaten at home by his father. His mother took the blame, so his father was still running a local business, playing golf at the weekends with friends and rarely visited Stuart. She remembers Roger, a little boy with Downs syndrome too; his father was a solicitor and was ashamed that they'd had a disabled child, so disowned Roger and told family and friends that they'd had a stillborn birth. Roger never had any visitors, but the nursing staff loved him and played with him, helping him to crawl. In fact, this story chimes with me. When my husband and I fostered we were asked to take Harry on to live with us when he was two months old. Harry had Downs syndrome and his parents disowned him when his mum Sadie gave birth and they saw that Harry was disabled. We took over from previous foster parents who found it difficult to cope with Harry when he took three hours more or less to drink a bottle of milk, as his lips sagged and he had a very weak suck. So, after an hour's break we had to start the next feed, day in and day out, with just a fairly short break to sleep each night. Balancing looking after Harry with our two other children aged three and five years old at the time was pretty challenging, despite my husband and I sharing the feeding duties – when I was home from my full-time job as a GP. Luckily Sadie re-assessed the motherly life she was missing and gave parenting a try with Harry after all- and as far as I know that did work out.

Large numbers of autistic people were held inappropriately in inpatient mental health hospitals, often isolated from their family, where their differences and needs were not understood or cared for. Autistic people are often misunderstood, judged and stigmatised as a result of society's lack of understanding and acceptance. While autism is not a mental health condition itself, these common, negative experiences can lead to them suffering from loneliness, burnout and poor mental health.

And now?

As I've been writing about the unkind and thoughtless ways that people with severe mental health conditions have been treated over the last century, it is good that in general our society nowadays is much more welcoming to people with disabilities like Downs syndrome or autism; and the stigma associated with an illegitimate pregnancy rarely features. There are still substantive problems though in our health service. With the numbers of beds for severely unwell patients being limited, it can be that someone in need of an emergency admission for an acute mental illness is transported to a vacant bed hundreds of miles away, making personal support from family and friends whilst they are staying in hospital very difficult, and being likely to slow down their recovery. Recent data published by NHS England showed that 380 patients were sent to a hospital out of their area in one particular month last year, for example. Of those, nearly three-fifths were placed more than 60 miles from their home where nearly half remained in that hospital for more than 30 days.

Electroconvulsive therapy (ECT) is still regarded as an effective medical treatment for people with severe, psychotic or treatment-resistant depression, even 80 years after it was first initiated. There are many constraints that limit the provision of ECT treatment in mental hospitals such as misinformation, stigma and the substantive concerns that clinicians have about the after-effects on patients' cognition. As an example, in my local mental health hospital, nurse Belle told me how effective the treatment was for a young man, Rob, aged 20 years old who was admitted to her mental health ward, and detained under the mental health act because he was severely self-neglected, with a significant weight loss. He had become very distressed after unexpectedly finding his roommate at the local University unfortunately hanging - and deceased. On admission he was doubly incontinent, and had to be fed and watered. Due to this he was given emergency ECT which was delivered the following day. He was prescribed the treatment twice weekly for six weeks. Within two treatments Rob began to 'wake up', eat and drink small amounts, and started to talk to staff. After completing the 12 ECT treatments he made a remarkable recovery leading to his discharge from hospital. Ten years on, Belle has never encountered Rob again, and so believes that his recovery continued and he went on to live his life independently. Over 30 patients per year still receive ECT therapy in any calendar year in the 2020s in this mental health hospital -with up to 12 treatments each. They do also provide some private care for patients referred from independent hospitals – which costs around £700 per treatment.

I wonder if we will look back in decades to come and view how we are treating people with severe dementia these days. When they need specialist nursing care rather than just residential care they will be likely to be locked in a section of the home without any way of going outside the building unless it is in their care plan and there are sufficient staff on duty to accompany them on a one-to-one basis, maybe with a connecting strap attached to them that the carer can hang on to. Is that much different from these asylum stories that I've reminisced about here?

And of course, these days the term 'asylum' is more likely to appear in newsprint or on TV to refer to the very many people who have travelled across the world from their own country, seeking sanctuary elsewhere. They have usually had to run for their lives owing to their fear of being punished for reasons such as their religion, nationality, ethnicity, political connections, and much more. In 2024, nearly 130,000 people were waiting for their applications for asylum in the UK to be decided (and many others had probably arrived illegally and stayed hidden from the authorities). But the official figures for immigration are sky high – with more than 1.2 million people described as 'immigrants' in the UK in 2022, but more than 500,000 people were also logged as having departed from the UK that year. So, this scaling up of the size of our population in the UK puts additional pressures on our NHS – as the size of our workforce, especially senior and experienced doctors, nurses and other registered clinicians, is not increasing proportionately, and those seeking asylum often have many health and wellbeing problems. Digital exclusion is a big factor among people seeking asylum and creates barriers to them accessing and using healthcare especially for their mental ill-health – if they do not have the tech device, Wi-Fi, language and digital skills needed. They have specific needs too that the UK healthcare system is not ready for – for instance, their lack of vaccinations could trigger outbreaks of infectious diseases, especially if those infected live in shared accommodation. Many asylum seekers are given accommodation in deprived areas, so this puts pressure on general practices, hospitals and other public services such as schools in those locations. GP practices should accept local residents as patients – that's a great facet of our NHS as they do not have any right to decline patient registration on the basis of race, age, gender, religion, social class, a disability or medical condition. A great example of the range of health services provided to asylum seekers is in my local area of Stoke-on-Trent, where teams from our local University Hospital of North Midlands have run breast and bowel cancer screening at ASHA, the voluntary, collaborative enterprise which serves around 600 local refugees and asylum seekers each week. The range of services includes guidance on how to register for, and access, online NHS and GP services, mental health screening and support – just what so many asylum seekers need.

Chapter 6. Whistleblowing, or not?

Fifty years on from my experience as a young doctor working at a Nottingham hospital, when I had a go at being a whistleblower, nothing much seems to have changed. When I started out in my first job as a junior doctor on a medical ward, I noticed that the consultant in charge seemed to be bonkers. If he heard an aeroplane flying overhead whilst he was leading the daily ward round, he instructed the team of four or so doctors to scatter around the ward, and duck under a bed or behind a door. We must have been quite close to an airport as this was a common occurrence – about once a week. The others in the team tolerated it and hid, and at first I joined in, as the other doctors in the team were more senior than me and I followed their lead. Then I decided to take action and tried to report Dr Edden to the senior doctors in the hospital who were termed 'the three wise men', sending a letter to their hospital secretary. They invited me to their next meeting in person and after I'd explained my concerns responded that 'We won't take any action against one of our own' (meaning their consultant colleague). They declined any more interaction with me, and the chair stood up, opened the door and saw me out with a very hostile frown. Because it was a sort of secret no personal action was taken against me; but Dr Edden went off sick soon after for the rest of the time that I was allotted to work on that ward – so at least one of the three wise men probably did talk to him about his situation and my concerns.

I've described in Chapter 7 the difficulties that I had about reporting my GP employer Dr D's suspected prescription fraud to the police or General Medical Council, because I needed substantive evidence and not just my strong suspicions. It has always been difficult to gather such objective evidence to support an allegation of wrong doing – and if a person admits to me that they have done wrong and honestly commits to changing their working ways or lifestyle habits, then I don't want the NHS to lose them from the workforce unnecessarily. Over the last 50 years of working in, and for, the NHS I've taken action a good few times after smelling alcohol on a doctor's or nurse's or manager's breath, whilst at work. When I worked for the NHS in the 1970s and early 1980s, it was common for junior doctors to drink alcohol whilst on duty, working 36 hours non-stop shifts in hospitals. There were no legal alcohol restrictions then either if they were driving home by car after their shift. I didn't drink alcohol at work like most of the male doctors did, so I often had to cover for drunken colleagues in the late evening when they'd been sitting in the doctors' mess between seeing patients, helping themselves from the doctors' bar and topping up the honesty payment box. It was only when I was a GP in Stone, that the partners decided around 1990 not to include alcohol in our staff Christmas lunchtime get togethers – before they went back to seeing patients in clinic an hour or so later. So anytime I've smelt alcohol on the breath of a staff member by chance when they've been talking to me in a patient setting, I've found a quiet time soon after in person, or by phone, to talk to them quietly about it. I'd explain that I didn't intend to report them officially if they would seek help voluntarily themselves, if they were not able to overcome their inappropriate drinking whilst on duty that could affect their patient care or management decisions. As far as I knew that always worked out well and I never detected follow-up alcohol drinking at work – though of course they might have dodged behind a wall and hid, seeing me coming! So, the outcomes were much better than whistleblowing on them.

A friend of mine, Ann, joined in reporting a senior ward nurse Mary to the hospital manager in the 1980s, because she bullied junior nurses all the time (Ann was one) on their general medicine ward. One of the main victims, Amy, who'd been treated appallingly, reported Mary to the hospital hierarchy and resigned from her post. The bully was moved to work in a cardiology ward and put onto a lower grade for a very short time and then a couple of months later reinstated into her previous senior nurse role. This was a very token response and unfair to the victim, Amy. A few years later Ann had switched to working as a nurse in general practice and remembers witnessing the practice manager Paul, drinking alcohol at his desk on duty and behaving irrationally as he was sloshed. Ann called one of the GPs through, who confronted the manager. Paul denied it but another staff member later found a vodka bottle in the bin; so, the nursing team pressured the GP partners to act and they did, giving him a written warning about drinking alcohol at work or he would lose his job. Paul amended his ways and apologised to Ann a few months later, who appreciated that.

I had another bitter taste of whistleblowing in 2007 – and I'm finding it very upsetting writing about it 17 years later! I applied for and got a lead post as Director of Postgraduate General Practice Education, at the NHS West Midlands Workforce Deanery. This was a prestigious job – one of 15 Directors or so across the UK, paid at about £120,000 p.a. from memory, an awful lot of money in those days. I was in charge of the training of hundreds of qualified doctors in their three-year specialty training based in medical posts in a range of NHS settings across the West Midlands, to become fully qualified GPs. I was employed by the West Midlands Strategic Health Authority (SHA) which had just been created by bringing together the sub-regional SHAs. So, I was no longer to be partly based in my local one, Shropshire and Staffordshire SHA with a headquarters 10 miles away from where I lived, but had to travel to Birmingham with a 96 miles round trip by car everyday, or suffer around 1.5 hours train travel from home and then back, as I had to change stops and go on two different trains to get to the Deanery base in Birmingham (and I couldn't claim these travel expenses back). Not a great travel arrangement but I got used to leaving home before 6.30am to avoid the worst motorway traffic and arrive at work at 8am or so. It was the same for my team – one member, Susan, had a disabled child and had agreed with her local SHA that she could work from home (unusual in those days!!) for three days a week so that she could be with her little boy aged three years old, before and after nursery. But when the West Midlands SHA took over our employment, the prior agreement was cancelled and Susan had to travel a 110 miles round trip to Birmingham every week day from her Shropshire home if she wanted to keep her job. Not a good start! I'd never been directly employed by NHS top management before and I was shocked by the management culture of *instruction* rather than *facilitation*. First of all, without any consultation I was put in charge of managing postgraduate training in nursing and dentistry as well as the general practice training programme contained in my job description. No discussion – and it doubled my workload and responsibilities. Then as I stood up to the top management over the next year or so to improve our GP training and stop them from pinching funds from our budget and divert the £s to pay for other workstreams without my agreement, I got hostile responses from the chief executive and head of nursing. I tried to confide my concerns about the poor management to the Chair of the board of the SHA – but again I was just put down. I continued to stand up to this disruptive management on behalf of my team and one day arrived at work on a Monday morning to find that they had hired workers to come into the building over the weekend and take the walls of my office down, so I no longer had a quiet and secluded location for private meetings or phone calls with struggling doctors in training, or their supervisors who needed to discuss highly confidential matters. I ended up trying to record the put down corridor conversations that these senior managers had with me, with a recording device stuffed in my bra, but if they drivelled on for more than 15 minutes I was worried that time was running out and it would start beeping. In the end I just resigned one day without any other job to move on to, when I couldn't put up with this toxic management any more – as I had a minimum three month notice period agreement in my contract. The chief executive told me to clear my desk and leave the building there and then; and brought a friend in to take an 'independent' statement from me about my decision to leave – and as I gave my views and perspectives I was told 'You don't really want to say that, do you?' I refused to quit that day and it took me at least 48 hours at my desk to review the many workstreams I had underway and ensure that the various elements and actions were allotted to deputies to lead on and sort out. The organisation did try to brief against me, and slur my name and reputation with the other UK Directors of Postgraduate General Practice Education, whom I met a month later at our annual event, as I was still employed for three months – albeit on a paid holiday by that time. I met up with the SHA lead nurse director several years later and he came across to me at a conference and held out his hand and apologised abjectly for how he and the SHA board had treated me. That meant a lot to me. And similarly, one of the other SHA managers moved up to Staffordshire as a chief executive of a local hospital trust a few years later and was terribly apologetic and wanted to work with me in my lead role in primary care – which we did, mending fences and putting the past behind us. But even recently when I was at a retired doctors' conference, I met Dr Bryan for the first time since I had resigned from my Director role 16 years earlier. He was still puzzled as to why I'd left that senior role as he and the other mid-level trainers in postgraduate education across the West Midlands had been waiting hopefully for me to transform the delivery of the GP specialty training programme, to match the needs of trainers and GP trainees. They had believed in me, and suddenly I'd disappeared, with lots of smears on my reputation from official messages indicating I'd got better things to do elsewhere, that I'd selfishly prioritised!

A top SHA manager moved on to a similar lead executive role soon after in another NHS related organisation, from which she was forced to resign a few years later following external investigations into performance shortcomings and doubts about cover ups in a hospital scandal; which then led to a public inquiry with lots of national interest and an official apology from the then Secretary of State for Health. At that time Sir Robert Francis led an independent review and called for an end to the culture of workplace bullying and fear in the NHS, so that staff could feel safe and be able to speak out. About time!!

The NHS does need whistleblowers – it's a shame that managers don't always appreciate that, and prefer to mask system failures, and safety concerns, and the accidental and purposeful mistakes by staff, as well as individuals' incompetence. Some whistleblowers do go public (like I'm doing now!), but many others accept pay-offs as part of compromise agreements - some of which have gagging clauses. Dr Phil Hammond reported in *Private Eye* in 2011 that the Treasury had approved 192 pay offs worth nearly £6 million across non-Foundation hospital trusts in England in 2008-2009. One specific example Phil gave in that article was of a consultant cardiac anaesthetist (Dr B) raising concerns in 1989 about a cardiac surgeon at Bristol Royal Infirmary (where I trained to be a GP in the late 1970s) who took far too long to complete his operations, leading to babies suffering from heart failure and brain damage that might have been averted. It took many years for the repeated raising of concerns about his practice to trigger a public inquiry that concluded that up to 35 children undergoing surgery before 1995 had died needlessly. Phil describes the brave whistleblower Dr B as having been 'ostracised and briefed against' by NHS managers, which drove him to emigrate to Australia. Once there, he took up a senior medical role in Australia in 1996 and extended his clinical role to an academic focus too, enabling him to contribute to the formation of international medical and ethical standards. The Health Secretary in 2001 told MPs that the anaesthetist, Dr B, 'is owed a debt of gratitude having been left with no option but to go to the media about the death of 29 babies at a UK hospital' – great that Dr B got that national recognition in the end and sacrificing his career as a consultant anaesthetist in Bristol was hopefully worth it; and there was a reported improvement in mortality rates for children's heart surgery in that hospital.

Dr Peter Wilmhurst is a well known whistleblower who never seems to have ceased standing up to the hostile attempts to shut him up for more than five decades. His first well known whistleblowing case was when he was working as a cardiologist at a hospital in London in 1986. He gathered substantiated evidence that a pharmaceutical company was falsifying data about the effectiveness, and masking safety risks, of their new heart drug. He won eventually and the drug was withdrawn from the market – an amazing success for an individual doctor to take on an international company at that scale. That whistleblowing part of Peter's character and his determination seems to have stuck with him throughout his working life, from what Wikipedia relays about him - continually publicising his medical concerns about patient treatments and exposing research misconduct and personal stories of how a few doctors, and others found guilty of wrongdoing, continue to retain their positions of power.

Chris Day is another ex-junior doctor who was a whistleblower about unsafe staffing levels in the Intensive Care Unit in the Queen Elizabeth hospital in London where he worked in 2014. He was made to cover extra wards when the two locum doctors expected to come into work did not turn up. His contract was ended and his training number cancelled so that he was unable to continue his postgraduate programme for his specialist training. Over ten years later his appeal is still in limbo as judgements favouring the Trust seem to have ignored issues, like the apparent shredding of documents that might have supported his case. There's been thousands of supporters who've helped Dr Day, by contributing to his legal costs via crowdfunding, that has enabled his appeal to continue.

And now?
Recently dozens of workers told Sky News of their unfair treatment after they spoke out about working in various NHS roles. The charity Protect relayed that two-thirds of those staff from all types of work settings who called their helpline that year, had been treated badly after speaking out. Most had shared their concerns with their NHS employers assuming that

they would take remedial action and improve the quality of care that they had been briefed about; they were shocked that they had then been victimised for being classed as 'whistleblowers'. Protect has some good news stories about whistleblowers that they've collated over the last 30 years.

One recent example of this scapegoating of doctors who speak out is the recent dismissal of two senior consultant surgeons who raised concerns about medical negligence, relating to dozens of deaths of patients (about 40) between 2015 and 2020 at a hospital in Brighton, with an ongoing police investigation now.

Jim was telling me how only last year he had worked as the deputy associate chief nurse overseeing the nursing workforce providing specialised neurological care spanning two linked hospitals in the region. One week, Jim flagged 'inadequate staffing' as a red/amber rating, but his manager instructed him to pretend that there'd been an improvement, and change the rating to green, prior to a CQC inspection that was about to happen. He refused to do so; and the senior management reacted by moving him to work on another ward as the lead nurse practitioner there. They'd moved him as a sort of punishment for refusing to cooperate and lie about the rating of a ward that was regarded as failing by other nurses too. His nurse manager openly grinned at him and laughed when she shifted him to work in the new ward and removed his deputy associate chief nurse status. So, he thought he'd no choice but to resign from that role that he'd held for four years, and take a new job based 200 miles away, even though this was disruptive for his family and he had a divorce underway and so still wanted to retain close connections with his kids. Jim told me that soon after his experience of this NHS management bullying, another male nurse in a similar senior nursing role on a different ward who would do anything to please senior managers, did agree to change his ward's score to a 'green rating' at the nurse manager's request, just to please the chief nurse of the hospital!

Gill, a medical student now at the same hospital in Nottingham where I trained 50 years ago, told me recently about how she had tried to report unacceptable behaviour by a surgeon who was her educational supervisor. She described how when this consultant taught female students he would 'automatically pat the girl on the knee if she gets one of his questions right saying 'good girl' in a patronising way.' Sometimes he asks female medical students to tie on his apron before surgery. When a male medical student was in the group too and saw the consultant behave like that, he said afterwards 'Gosh, that was bad!' Gill reported the consultant to her educational supervisor and apparently he got a 'talking to' about his sexist behaviour, but he still carries on in the same way when teaching female medical students, without any repercussions (yet!!).

I read recently how an NHS whistleblower aged 30 years old has sacrificed his career as an emergency medical technician for the ambulance service, by capturing on a hidden camera, several needless deaths in the back of his ambulance. He wore hidden cameras and microphones whilst working on shift to film example patients whose safety was definitely at risk, to try and trigger system improvement. He filmed patients over a period of two months in mid-winter in a way that concealed their identities, with many of their faces blurred. He captured appalling conditions inside the emergency departments in local hospitals where corridors were stacked with patients for many hours, and ambulances were stuck in queues outside in the car parks with their patients lying waiting for emergency care from hospital staff and their condition deteriorating.

Mind you, there's been recent publicity given to an MP calling for social workers to carry body cams to discreetly identify and record domestic abuse. He recommended that children's social workers could be set up to wear cameras to spot signs of such abuse so that they could capture photographic evidence when out and about at work, rather than rely on 'hearsay' evidence.

Two of the hospitals that have been in the news headlines recently for their intolerance of whistleblowers are the Heartlands hospital and the Queen Elizabeth hospital which are part of the University Hospitals Birmingham (UHB) Trust. The Hospital Trust has been heavily criticised for its toxic bullying culture and poor governance that has made doctors and nurses employed by the Trust wary about speaking up, putting patients' care and wellbeing at risk. There had been public concerns about the quality of patient care at the Trust over the preceding years, with an eye specialist for example winning an employment tribunal for wrongful dismissal by the Trust in 2017, when he raised concerns about a lack of nurses available to support operations.

Such whistleblowing can wreck the person's career, even if they win their case. A former medical director for the Isle of Man apparently won more than £3 million compensation recently, but describes the case as having shattered her 35 year medical career. She was pushed out of her job after raising concerns about patient safety, and a lack of governance, relating to the pre-emptive precautions that she had tried to set up to prevent Covid infections overwhelming the health care services on the island. The Hospital Trust hierarchy had described the doctor as being unfit for the job that the island's chief executive had shifted her to. On this occasion the whistleblower won – but only sort of, as her career was destroyed and the NHS lost an effective medical director by the sound of it.

The bullying and harassment that I had experienced from senior staff whilst working in the West Midlands Strategic Health Authority (SHA) in the two years that I was employed there in 2006-2007 still seems to be a common feature in the NHS, drawing on a report of staff perspectives which was published in 2021. Around 19% of staff reportedly experienced bullying, harassment or abuse from colleagues, 12% described such behaviour from managers and 28% from patients, relatives and members of the public, with at least 5% of nurses who were leaving the profession citing bullying as their reason for quitting their job. Other issues arising from this seeming tolerance of bullying and harassment in the NHS at all levels, and the toxic atmosphere this creates in the organisation, are the effects on individual clinicians and other staff, so that they are more likely to commit errors and deliver worse patient care when working within a culture of fear, along with higher rates of absenteeism and poorer productivity.

This tells us that the NHS is in dire need of a fundamental culture change. A sad example of how NHS management is still ignoring workforce concerns that are relayed to them, came from Dan recently. He was a senior nurse manager whom I met when he worked part-time for NHS commissioners alongside his hospital employed nurse manager post. He had redesigned the framework of intermediate care (care pitched between hospital and home settings for patients who still needed active nursing and medical follow-on care) in 2016. Intermediate care nurses would ring round care homes every morning to see which residents were likely to need additional care soon; then provide upfront nursing care and sort out the medical issues proactively. This approach reduced hospital admissions by one-third and got a national award in 2017; the only extra costs were the new care home matron post and the intermediate care clinicians working in the community. Then the commissioners switched to a different provider of the service without any consultation with Dan or the intermediate care team; with no tendering for competing care providers to be paid for delivering the ongoing service, as far as Dan knows. The lead commissioner told Dan 'not to interfere and treat providers of care like adults'. The new service failed...and the top commissioning managers blamed Dan as the scapegoat even though he had not been in a position to enable him to take system-wide responsibility for deciding on the new provider. He was told by a senior commissioner 'You've pissed someone off. I can't tell you who, but you'd better get another role' – so he did. Another loss to the NHS as he went to work for a private provider elsewhere.

I was telling an old friend, Dave, about my experiences of standing up to hostile, bullying NHS managers the other day and he relayed how he had experienced some similar episodes in his long nursing career. Like me, Dave has always had high ethical standards and behaviour, and prides himself on being fair to people, whatever their status – staff and patients or their carers. He described never feeling inferior or superior to other people whatever their seniority or lower rank and sees himself as a team member, not a boss. Over the years he's learnt to adopt a quirky approach to senior figures who are trying to bully him, as I have done, rather than get into a confrontation and he'll try to disarm their negativity. He's immensely grateful to those who've inspired him over his clinical career; and tries to model the behaviour that he admires.

That's been my approach too. I've always tried to chair NHS or academic meetings over the years with a facilitatory approach, indicating that everyone's welcome to give us an update and contribute their truthful views and insights and do not need to fear that their bosses or colleagues or those outside the organisation will take umbrage with them. This was particularly hard work when I was an NHS leader, chairing our local Clinical Commissioning Group (CCG) in Stoke-on-Trent in 2016-2018. We had bi-monthly meetings with local MPs and other local leaders who thought that this was their opportunity to jab the knife into the NHS managers who were just overseeing the delivery of care services that government ministers demanded. So, there was no point in the MPs (a mix of Labour and Conservatives) screeching about the £millions fines that the local Hospital Trust had to pay back to the CCG because they had not met deadline targets like waiting times in A&E or discharging patients from hospital. Those fines were imposed by the government, and the MPs instead of literally pointing aggressively and screaming at our chief executive about the fines, should have intelligently discussed how we needed to enable the local Hospital Trust to improve and provide the best care for their constituents, and thus not be allotted future fines imposed by the government.

A recent review has considered if the NHS in England is safer now, more than a decade after the Francis review. The Francis report into the serious failings at the Mid-Staffordshire NHS Foundation Trust in 2013 was very insightful. It relayed the 'appalling suffering of so many patients', and how the Hospital Trust board members had not listened sufficiently to its staff and patients who had reported their concerns about the many hundreds of patients found to have died from the poor care that they received between 2005 and 2009. The report authors recognised how Hospital Trust bosses had prioritised reaching national access targets and financial balance, over and above delivering consistently good standards of health care; and they had ignored warning signs and dodged accountability by disengaging from their managerial and leadership responsibilities. The Francis report recommended that a 'Freedom to Speak Up' guardian be appointed in every NHS Trust to support staff.

The proportion of NHS organisations judged at CQC visits as being 'good' or 'outstanding' as regards patient safety has risen since 2014. Nearly half of staff surveyed by the CQC though describe that they do not feel confident that they'll be treated fairly if they report any concerns to their managers, and many staff, patients and carers feel that there is a failure for anyone to really listen if they voice concerns – they are regarded as nuisances.

An NHS whistleblowing scheme was rolled out across England in 2019 to support staff who raise the alarm about their concerns as to unsafe practice at their workplace. One reason for the scheme being created was to show staff it is okay to raise concerns and not be deterred from coming forward because they fear the consequences. It includes support for members of the public too who can experience defensive, and sometimes rude, responses when they make complaints about their care, as the NHS wants to be seen to create an open and honest complaints culture for patients.

An annual report on whistleblowing disclosures published by NHS England, found that there were 110 whistleblowing disclosures made from general practices and other primary care organisations in the 12 months period up to March 2022, and 96 made from staff working in hospitals. These mainly related to examples of poor patient safety in relation to clinical practice, concerns about clinical or information governance, and the conduct of other employees or leaders in their employing Trust. The NHS 'Freedom to Speak Up' team took action in around two-thirds of cases; that included delving deeper to gather more information or referring the NHS Trust or primary care organisation employing the staff whistleblower to another body to investigate, such as the Care Quality Commission or regulatory bodies. The 'Freedom to Speak Up' ethos is currently being actively pushed by the NHS at a national level; to change the culture so that workers know how to speak up and raise concerns about risk, malpractice or wrongdoing, and feel safe and encouraged to do so. NHS organisations must identify and tackle barriers to staff speaking up, without there being any retaliation or detriment to them, and the individual staff who speak up are not bullied, excluded or treated negatively.

A recent report drawn up from the NHS Staff Survey of 2022, in which 264 NHS organisations took part, (comprising acute and mental health hospital Trusts, ambulance Trusts, community and specialist Trusts, social enterprises and management bodies but not primary care staff such as those working in general practices, or dental or pharmacy or optometry settings) had 636,348 staff responding to the survey (a 93% response rate!). Many staff responding described being disillusioned about speaking up and felt that to do so would be 'futile' and put themselves at risk. Less than three-quarters of staff felt secure about raising their concerns about unsafe clinical practice, and only just over half of respondents were confident that their NHS organisation would address their concerns and improve the service. About one in six staff reported experiencing at least one incident of physical violence in the previous year – from patients or their relatives, or other members of the public; and nearly half described being harassed or bullied by patients or their relatives or members of the public, and/or from managers or other colleagues. The majority of respondents were frontline staff such as registered nurses, midwives, nursing or healthcare assistants, medical and dental staff. So, it looks as though not much has changed in relation to the culture of bullying and harassment in the NHS that I experienced in my senior role 15 years earlier.

Recent guidance on 'good medical practice' by the General Medical Council (GMC) is very clear that doctors must keep patients safe by for example, reporting any suspected adverse drug reactions, relaying concerns about another doctor's fitness to practise to a colleague, their medical defence body or the GMC. So that cover up by the government and NHS in hiding the truth from 30,000 or so people across the UK that they had been infected by blood products or transfusions cannot happen again – we need whistleblowers who believe that the powers that be will listen to them, investigate their concerns in a fair and balanced way, and praise them for coming forward – not punish or degrade them as a result.

The current NHS national guardian recently highlighted that only 71% of NHS workers recently surveyed, feel secure about raising concerns about unsafe clinical practice in the NHS setting that they work in. Most of these were confident that their organisation would act to address their expressed concerns; with three out of five staff confirming that their organisation had taken action to ensure that reported errors, or near misses, or incidents do not happen again. Medical professionals were reportedly the least confident about speaking out in this national NHS staff survey. Not much has changed then!

So, the last word on the importance of respecting and listening to whistleblowers goes to the British Medical Association (BMA) UK Council chair, Professor Phil Banfield. He told delegates at their annual conference recently that doctors are 'fighting back' to improve patient care, battle against years of pay erosion and stem the tide of colleagues leaving the country. "As well as standing up for the institution, we must also stand up for those who call it out when it fails. I promise you, today, that the BMA will not stand by as employers try to silence those who raise concerns…..there are brave doctors who take a stand and speak out in this chaos. Yet, whistleblowers are continuously undermined or disciplined or sacked. They are pilloried because some NHS organisations believe that the reputational hit is more dangerous than unsafe care."

I very much agree. Everyone should feel able to speak up, and the NHS must find ways to allow and encourage people to do so, in supported ways. The potential whistleblower should not feel that they must choose between protecting patient safety, or risking their own career and livelihood.

Chapter 7. Dispensing with(in) the rules!

The day when my university application had to be submitted I had still not made up my mind what course or university to apply for. Should it be for medicine or pharmacy – or both? I was considering pharmacy because my father had asked a friend at his golf club to give me a job at his local pharmacy in my school holidays when I was 17 years old (in the late 1960s). That was an eye opener for me about the possibility of my becoming a pharmacist – and it was my first paid job and lasted for five weeks. After a couple of days of my serving on the counter, the dispenser who did the bulk of the pharmacy work sorting the paper-based prescriptions that people brought in from their doctors, asked me to help out. So, without any training or checks as to my competence or trustworthiness, I was counting out the exact numbers of tablets and pouring specific quantities of liquid medicines into glass bottles, as detailed in the wodge of paper prescriptions that were piled up in order by the counter staff – a bit like ordering your drinks in a queue of customers in a coffee shop these days. No-one checked that I'd selected the right medication or measured the right quantity of liquid medicines or counted out the tablets correctly. When the dispenser realised that he could delegate to me and just go off into a back room and read a newspaper, he did so – day after day. His boss, the fully trained pharmacist buzzed between the many pharmacies he owned and the golf course – we hardly ever saw him. So, there I was acting as a pharmacist, doing a job that it would take four years to train for at university these days. I declined to answer the customers' personal queries though about their health conditions, or the medicines that they were taking!

In the mid-1990s there were around 1,200 dispensing general practices in England and Wales, which together dispensed about 35 million items per year for their own registered patients. These were mainly based in rural communities, where it might otherwise be difficult for patients to access the medication prescribed by their GPs; as community pharmacies were mainly based in busy town centres with lots of retail products on sale alongside. There are far fewer dispensing general practices today. And it was with a dispensing practice in a little rural village that I took on my first post-training GP role in the early 1980s as a salaried GP, employed by Dr D who owned the practice. Patient care was provided by Dr D and me, with a nurse who worked half-time and a receptionist who also doubled up with a practice management role. We had about 2,300 registered patients for whom we provided medical care night and day; with equal shares of covering out-of-hours care for any of our patients each evening and night, and alternate weekends.

Our GP surgery was in a very small building with only one doctor's consulting room, so Dr D and I took it in turns to be the on-site GP. The patients usually started queuing outside the practice for an appointment that day from 8am. One of us started at 9am and saw the queuing patients between 9am to 11am, allowing about five minutes for each patient, after which around ten more patients were booked in so that we could start doing the requested home visits at midday - usually about six or so over a five miles range. Gradually a new pattern started – when I was in as the main doctor there'd be a queue of patients outside and down the street by 9am; when Dr D was the on-site doctor there'd be one or two patients standing at the entry door. I tended to listen to patients – whereas he usually jumped straight into telling them what he thought was wrong with them and what treatment he was giving them. We started our next surgery again about 3pm with more booked patients until we'd finish around 6pm. In between we'd be dispensing medication or overseeing the receptionist who was helping out with this, and writing up notes on our paper medical records, and catching up with pharmaceutical representatives (we called them 'drug reps' then) – who came along to see us at the practice surgery, to persuade us that their drug was better than their rivals' for a specific clinical purpose, such as helping people to keep their blood pressure down.

When I finished seeing patients and writing up my notes or organising referral letters at the end of my working day, I transferred any incoming telephone calls from the practice base to my phone at home, about 15 minutes drive away. If a patient phoned in for advice or to request a home visit, they left a message and I'd call back, if I wasn't at home in person to take the call – or if my husband was in, he'd take the call and patients would be telling this strange man all of their personal confidential details for him to pass on to me, their on-call GP. If Dr D was away on holiday for three weeks abroad with his family (as he liked to do twice a year), I was on call for 24 hours a day for all that time without a break whilst running the morning and afternoon surgeries every weekday too.

I gradually started to wonder whether there was prescription fraud going on in the practice. It was common for Dr D to have 15 minutes private chats in the car park with pharmaceutical reps and then there'd be a swop with Dr D carrying in boxes of drugs to stack up inside the surgery, having clinched the deals at a lower price for buying in bulk no doubt. He'd push me to give a patient a specific drug (that he'd bought as a cheap deal in the car park presumably) or several types of medication at once, for any minor illness like tonsillitis – antibiotics, pain killers, cough medicine, lozenges etc.; and was pretty cross if I refused and went for just the medication that I judged the patient needed. Patients would come back to see me for a follow-up consultation bringing back armfuls of drugs that they didn't need and left in reception, to be re-allocated to another patient in future. That meant that Dr D got paid twice by the Prescription Prescribing Authority for the same medication. When he spotted that a packet of tablets stacked on the shelf in the office had gone out of date, Dr D would put them on our doctor's desk to prompt us to prescribe that pack as soon as possible and find any old patient for them, even if their allocation was not really justified by their health condition.

One morning, I gave Dr D three months notice that I was resigning as his salaried GP and told him why – that I had gradually realised that there was prescription fraud going on and I did not want any part in it. He threatened me in an angry way when I said I was prepared to take action and report him to the police and the General Medical Council, that registers doctors as being fit to practise. But I knew it was not the right time for me to report suspected fraud as I hadn't got any objective evidence, just strong suspicions, and I couldn't ask the individual practice staff to get involved. I had recently realised that Dr D had made them complicit in other practice-related fraud, such as certifying that the number of hours they worked was far more than they really did each week. In those days, a GP could reclaim 70% of paid support staff hours from the NHS, so Dr D was presumably making a fraudulent profit from this arrangement too. I did happen to meet the practice nurse at an educational event a few years later, who by that time had switched to working in another general practice. She insisted on telling me her version of events, and clarified that my suspicions about Dr D committing prescription fraud were correct. But she declined my suggestion to take it any further by informing the police or the General Medical Council. Dr D must have had quite a reputation outside our practice too; when I applied for a job in one of the neighbouring practices, they declined to accept my application, telling me that they feared he would be 'vituperative' if they were to appoint me as one of their GPs. That was the first time I'd heard the word 'vituperative' used (defined as 'bitterly abusive' in the dictionary I've just flicked through); but I've recognised that behaviour a few times since, when I've successfully stood up to disconnected NHS leads.

Ten or so years later I heard informally from a friend that the Department of Health was seeking a clinical adviser on prescription fraud. I applied and was interviewed by phone. I reeled off some of my insights and examples of prescription fraud that I believed that I'd witnessed and they immediately took me on. We took a year or so collating our case studies and evidence of prescription fraud across England and Wales to evolve the 'Efficiency Scrutiny into Prescription Fraud' report which was published in 1997 by the NHS Executive. That was my first experience of working at a top national level, reporting in person to the Cabinet Office in Downing Street. We had two remits: 'to assess the scale of fraudulent and incorrect claims for exemption by NHS patients liable to pay prescription charges'; and 'to assess the scale of fraud and irregularity by contractors who issue NHS prescriptions and/or dispense drugs or other items prescribed.'

Fraud can be opportunistic if someone makes dishonest gains when there are opportunities to do so. Fraud involves criminal deception when the person knows that they are breaking the law, to generate those gains for their own benefit. Sometimes the rules might be broken by a doctor say, without personal gain, for the convenience of their patients. A pharmacy contractor would be committing fraud if they were claiming reimbursement for prescription medications which were not actually dispensed and given to the patient. Prescription forms might be seen as blank cheques which could be exchanged for goods worth hundreds of pounds. Sometime this might be by collusion with a local doctor whose

patient it was e.g. the GP wrote a batch of inaccurate prescriptions approved by the NHS, for the pharmacist to be able to dispense a more effective type of medication not funded by the NHS in primary care.
This might be a short cut to obtain a specific medication or novel type of wound dressing say, already in use in hospitals but not yet on the drug tariff of items that could be prescribed by a GP. Thus, the GP would write a prescription for a quantity of permitted dressings of similar cost to the new type, and agree with the pharmacist that they would swop that for the off-tariff item instead.

In the old days (hopefully not now!) hospital consultants might be in drug companies' *pockets* too. Ken told me that when he was a ward nurse in a local hospital in the 1990s, he noticed one of the consultants using nebulised steroids for treating patients with a chronic lung disease (when the consultant was obliging a local pharmaceutical rep), although research showed that much cheaper inhalers were just as effective.
He did try to report the consultant to the hospital hierarchy then but he couldn't find anyone who'd listen to whom he could report his concerns.

One type of prescription fraud that still seems to often happen today, is if a particular patient, or a care home on their behalf, updates the pharmacy that regularly delivers the prescribed repeat drugs to their home, that they do not need to take 'as required' medication everyday all day, such as paracetamol or stronger painkillers – so please can they not dispense or deliver it automatically, each month. But the pharmacy may ignore this message and supply the whole lot each month. Recently, one of my friends Fiona told me that her work colleagues called her the 'drug mule' as if anyone wanted some pain killers for themselves or a close family member, they'd ask Fiona to bring them some free, that she'd been collecting from her mum's house every couple of months in large bags. Fiona had updated the local pharmacist many times that her mum rarely took her 'as required' prescription drugs but they declined to accept bags full of returns. But they insisted that they keep delivering the whole batch to her mum's home (because they were paid for dispensing each lot of medication and would lose their income if they did not keep providing them).

Prescription related fraud by GPs and pharmacists proved extremely difficult to detect during our 'Efficiency Scrutiny' in the mid-1990s, and often cases came to light through tip-offs from staff with insider knowledge – similar to the insights that I'd shared from working with Dr D. One of these tip offs I still remember was a pharmacist in Birmingham who was well known by young mothers as being prepared to switch a packet of nappies on sale in his pharmacy store, for a prescription that they obtained from their GP, by patients falsely claiming that they had symptoms that needed treatment, like depression.

The pharmacist made sure that he gave out packs of nappies worth about half or less of the cost of the various anti-depressants in the swop, so a nice profit for him from the costs of the medication and his dispensing services that he reclaimed from the NHS, even though he had not issued those anti-depressant drugs and had just given the packs of nappies as a trade off. We did get the police involved on that one!

In 1997 annual losses from prescription fraud were estimated to be up to £100 million from patients evading prescription charges, around £30million from theft and forgery of paper-based prescription forms, and an unspecified amount from contractor fraud (prescribing/dispensing doctors, and pharmacists). We found that 'the great majority of health care staff – whether they be doctors, pharmacists or support staff in the surgeries and pharmacies – were highly committed and honest.' We saw the future as being to move from an archaic manual system, to electronic prescribing which would reduce the risks of fraud, as well as produce clinical benefits by linking prescribing of medication to current clinical information, that would then improve the quality of the prescribing process. Doctors might still use handwritten forms though, for instance, on home visits to their patients as it took a good few years before it was usual for a GP to carry a dedicated tech device connected to patients' medical records, with them when away from their surgery on home visits to their patients.

Much of my own insights into how important it is to help patients to understand why and how they should take their prescribed medication according to the 'instructions' given by their doctor or nurse (sometimes called *shared decision making* by the clinician!!) comes from my experience of being given antiepileptic therapy as a teenager. My father wouldn't accept that I had been diagnosed as having epilepsy - around the age of 12 years old after several in-depth neurology consultations and testing. I'd been having 'fits' several times a year for at least five years, but my parents only took me to see a doctor because Carol my girl guides' leader insisted that they did so after I had a fit whilst away for a week at the summer girl guides camp. I was investigated twice but the diagnosis was the same – epilepsy. And so, I was prescribed an anticonvulsant medication by our GP. But I valued my father's perspective more than those of the specialist neurologist and our GP and I similarly denied that there was anything wrong with me.

To please my Mum I pretended to take the anticonvulsant treatment each day and usually chucked a few tablets at a time down a drain on my way to school. The exact diagnosis was not discussed with me as a teenager, so I only found out that I was thought to have epilepsy when I was 26 years old, and read my own medical records whilst the doctor I was seeing about my first pregnancy was holding up my records and asked for an update about my fits. I had to inform the DVLA retrospectively that I had been diagnosed with epilepsy; and then had a three-yearly renewal of my driving licence for a couple of decades. But in the end, I think my Dad was right and rather than having epilepsy I was having vasovagal fits which were triggered by sharp pain from knocking my knee or elbow or other body part. It's complicated!

> YOU OUGHT TO RETURN THESE. IF WORD GOT OUT YOU HAD THESE STASHED AWAY, THEIR STREET VALUE WOULD MAKE YOU A PRIME TARGET FOR A BURGLAR.

Prescription charges can be a barrier to keeping people well and in work – even in our relatively affluent country! These days, nearly one in ten people in England are thought to skip renewing their prescribed NHS medication due to the cost of prescriptions, and another 10% who pay for their prescriptions report cutting their medication in half, to make it last longer. People not being able to afford their prescribed medication has also led to them being more likely to have untreated mental health issues and increase the time they take off work with ill-health. If people with long-term health conditions cannot afford their medications and stop taking them, that triggers an increase in them making GP visits, trips to accident and emergency (A&E) departments and hospital stays – so costing the NHS much more than the basic costs of their missed medication. Irene is a bad example of this; she had been told that she had raised blood pressure for six years, and that she should take regular medication and lose weight as her body mass index put her in the 'obese' category. She was prescribed medication to bring her blood pressure down but she didn't take the tablets after a short while because the cost of paying for two prescriptions per month was so prohibitive and she believed that if she practised faith healing that would be more effective for her health and wellbeing, than taking pills. Sadly, Irene died last week at the age of 57 years after having a sudden brain haemorrhage out of the blue; her husband was with her when one side of her face became paralysed and she then lost consciousness. A 999 ambulance rushed her to hospital where they found that the bleed was so extensive that it was inoperable and she died a few hours later. Had she adopted a more healthy lifestyle and taken her prescribed medication regularly, she would have been likely to live for many more years with a well-controlled blood pressure.

England is the only UK country where people have to pay for their medicines – creating yet more health inequalities that England's politicians could reverse. As a GP working in a deprived area until recently, I often witnessed patients telling me they'd have to wait for their next pay day before they could afford to collect their prescription that we'd just issued for them for an acute infection, from the pharmacist, as they had no spare money. Then I'd go to a cupboard in my consulting room and see if I'd left any returned medication in there that I could donate to them for free. So, I was complicit to some extent - but I didn't rate this as 'prescription fraud' as I gained nothing and the patient could accelerate their treatment and hopefully not need to take that prescription to the pharmacist and pay for it, if they'd improved sufficiently from taking some of the stash of medication that I'd kept to hand to redistribute.

Complementary and alternative medicine treatments are often used as a replacement for, or as an adjunct to, conventional medicine and healthcare. NHS treatments are based on 'evidence based' medicine that is derived from reliable research evidence, the clinician's experiences and patient values. For instance, there are various herbal remedies for a range of health conditions where usage is supported by at least some reasonable evidence e.g. St John's Wort for depression or red clover for menopausal symptoms. As more and more research has been undertaken into the benefits of various alternative remedies, the scientific evidence emerging over the last 20 years has been unimpressive and thus has not met the criteria for being adopted by the NHS at scale, if it cannot be classed as 'effective' treatments. We have a National Institute for Health and Care Excellence (NICE) that was set up in 1999 and delivers a wide range of quality guidance and pathways across clinical and health conditions; the National Prescribing Centre merged with NICE in 2011. I've just searched at random on the NICE website as to their perspectives and guidance on St John's Wort now, in 2024. The advice is: 'Although there is evidence that St John's Wort may be of benefit in less severe depression, healthcare professionals should:

- advise people with depression of the different potencies of the preparations available and ... potential serious interactions .... with other drugs
- not prescribe or advise its use by people with depression because of uncertainty about appropriate doses, persistence of effect......'

I became increasingly interested in the evidence for complementary and alternative medicines in the 1990s and joined the evolving Foundation for Integrated Medicine. As a Board member I was invited with my husband to an exclusive dinner held in Highgrove in 2000 with the then Prince Charles as host and main speaker. The College of Medicine succeeded the Foundation for Integrated Medicine in 2010 to 'bring together a patchwork of much broader ideas – from food and exercise, to new science, patient empowerment and integrated health.......to bring people together to create a more compassionate, progressive, value-based, sustainable healthcare system.' I was a member of its Scientific Committee for a good few years and it continued progressing and extending its scope to include many integrative, conventional, functional, lifestyle, complementary and holistic doctors, nutritionists and practitioners, focusing on whole-person, patient-centred health. We sometimes had special meetings at Clarence House in London near Buckingham Palace too and Highgrove again (e.g. there was a fantastic event in Highgrove gardens for around 40 of us; we had a spectacular trip around the gardens and then met personally with Prince Charles in small groups to discuss mutual interests in progressing integrative care). King Charles III has openly supported the adoption of alternative medicine as a norm for decades, based on 'personal, emotional, political and societal levels' of justification, rather than just the clinical evidence underpinning NICE guidance. That clash in thinking is captured in the NICE guidance on the use of St John's Wort by clinicians, as described above. The College of Medicine and Integrated Care is chaired by Dr Michael Dixon OBE, a country GP in Cullompton, who was also a health adviser to HRH The Prince of Wales (as was) for several decades and is now current head of the Royal Medical Household for King Charles. My personal view is that there is insufficient scientific evidence for many alternative therapies and medicines. So, individuals should balance the risks and benefits that they read up on, and give a particular remedy a go, if it seems to be recommended by reliable people or organisations, for their particular condition or circumstances.

In 2015 I tried (but did not succeed) to improve the safety of medication openly available to the general public for purchase over the counter. When I was in a bargain shop one day I noticed that they were selling three packets of paracetamol (48 tablets) for the price of two packs (32 tablets), for £1. This breached the recommended limit set by the Medicines and Healthcare products Regulatory Agency national guidelines for over-the-counter sales of aspirin and paracetamol, in particular for no more than 32 paracetamol 500mg to be sold in one batch at any shop/pharmacy without a person providing a prescription issued by a doctor. Pharmacies can issue 100 paracetamol 500mg or aspirin 75mg or 300mg tablets at a time with a prescription, or if the registered pharmacist deems it fitting to do so. To test things out I bought six packets (that is 96 paracetamol 500mg tablets) in one sale at Poundland with the cashier putting it through the till twice for the single payment of £2.

So, I recruited a lead medical student from Keele University and he got ten other students on board and they did an organised mystery shopping programme of how much paracetamol or aspirin they could buy as one purchase, in around 200 retail stores across Staffordshire and Shropshire over the following three months. One student for example, bought 14 packets x 16 paracetamol 500mg tablets (that's a total of 224 tablets, or seven times the recommended limit for the maximum amount that should be sold to the public) as one purchase. Thirteen of the stores sold illegal quantities of aspirin or paracetamol to a student by selling more than 100 tablet/capsules/caplets in one transaction.

All of these medical students were aware how common it is for a patient to die from an intentional paracetamol or aspirin overdose; and that for those who survive it is pretty common that their liver is damaged so much so that they require a liver transplant as a result. I worked with the lead student to capture this evidence and we managed to get the report published as a main paper in the esteemed national British Medical Journal.

Once it was published we approached local psychiatric consultants and national NHS and public health leads. But we were not able to motivate or shame those national leaders into pushing for a change to the law and so retail stores may still sell more than 32 tablets of paracetamol 500mg or aspirin 75mg, or 300mg, to a shopper at a time. So, we failed to make a national change to enforce the limit on selling these potentially dangerous drugs! Those medical students are ambassadors for change though, and I'm still watching for an opportunity to get publicity for this scandalous risk that still persists, whereby vulnerable people can make bulk buys of paracetamol and other medication, that can potentially do them harm if they overdose.

Mind you there are other medications you can buy over-the-counter or through online pharmacy suppliers these days that are considered unsafe, or are sold for conditions for which they are not licensed. It's pretty quick and easy to buy melatonin online for insomnia say, though it is described in the British National Formulary as a 'prescription only medicine'. I have just clicked on an online medication provider and asked if I can get a prescription for melatonin for insomnia linked to jet lag, from a doctor, before placing my order. But all I needed to do was complete an online assessment – and pay upfront (£30 for 30 melatonin 3mg tablets). Cannabis-based medicines are another example of a casual line between a patient needing an NHS prescription, for say easing the symptoms of epilepsy or muscle spasms, via a standard route such as a prescription from their hospital specialist, and bypassing the usual care pathway and obtain it privately in person or online.

The Association of the British Pharmaceutical Industry (ABPI) is the trade association set up in 1891 for companies in the UK producing prescription medicines. Its Code of Practice covers the promotion of medicines for prescribing to health professionals and administrative staff, as well as providing information for the UK public about prescription-only medicines. Over the decades their Code has become stricter. Decades ago, it was common for a pharmaceutical company to encourage their reps to organise and pay for lunches or evening suppers for teams of doctors at local restaurants, or conferences; or even to fund doctors to go abroad to attend an international conference that focused on clinical conditions like heart disease, that – guess what? - was one of the main retail streams that their company's drugs served. That meant that the doctor got their travel, hotel and conference funded; and there was no specific contract agreeing future prescribing behaviour. But there was research in the 1990s that found that most authors of academic papers describing the efficacy of a particular class of drug had received funding or freebies from the manufacturer, compared with just over a third of authors of published academic papers who were critical of the drug. When confronted with this evidence many of those doctors and academics who had accepted such inducements were shocked to realise that they may not have been as impartial as they'd thought. It was common for drug reps to visit GP surgeries, so there might be one popping into my consultation room at the end of most morning's surgeries – with gifts like pens, diaries, clocks, USB sticks, magnifying glasses and other useful goodies – which meant that you kept their gifts on your desk and couldn't avoid looking at their logo or message. They'd often bribe the receptionist to let them into individual GP's consulting rooms with special gifts like chocolates.

I did gain from the generosity of pharmaceutical companies, as several would buy thousands of the many books that I wrote on clinical practice for GPs and nurses each year. As they bulk bought them from my publisher Radcliffe Medical Press, I only got limited royalties – but I did get a well known reputation as a medical author as wherever I went - to a general practice or medical library across the UK – there were many of my books (not all were unopened, some looked like they had actually been read by doctors and nurses!!). The updated Code nowadays means that drug reps are restricted to a £5 limit per doctor with whom they interact – so no more free dinners or books! Regulations and governance are much tighter these days for pharmaceutical companies to allocate funding to NHS projects; but it is still possible for doctors and academics to successfully apply for grants or funding via 'joint working agreements', as I still do with local NHS organisations. In the past year I've successfully applied for funding from three major pharma companies to undertake quality improvement programmes that benefit patient care; those patients newly diagnosed or better managed will now receive more prescribed medication – though that is not necessarily linked to the specific medication produced by the sponsoring pharma company.

And now?

Commercial sales of pharmaceutical treatments are abounding these days. In a newspaper I was reading today is an advert for collagen – with the sales pitch being supported by reference to a professor in America who is seemingly verifying its use for arthritis. The promotion of the product refers to the previous assumption that using collagen helped to improve someone's wrinkles, and that now '8.5 million UK Arthritis sufferers' could use it as a supplement to help their arthritic knees or other joints and get a positive outcome after only taking it for two weeks. Really??!!

The prescription charge is £9.90 per item now in England unless a person buys a prepayment certificate upfront for three or twelve months with a slight reduction in bulk buying costs. There are a few good deals though, like the recent introduction of a 12 months prescription prepayment certificate for hormone replacement therapy which has been priced at £19.80. However, around 90% of prescriptions in England are provided free of charge – in line with people's circumstances, age, type of health condition, and income. These are a lifeline for many, with 15% or so of adults in England taking five or more medicines a day for their multiple health problems – described as polypharmacy. But according to a recent report from Age UK, more than one in five people in their fifties in England are worried about not being able to afford their prescriptions – but this burden has not been dumped on those living in Scotland, Northern Ireland and Wales, where prescriptions are still free for all age groups.

The number of prescriptions dispensed in the community in England shot up by 66% to 1.14 billion in 2021/22 from 686 million prescriptions per year in 2004/5. There are concerns about overprescribing – such as of antidepressant use – when such medication is thought to be essential for those with severe depression, but other types of treatment such as cognitive behaviour therapy might be substituted for medication and given a try for people with mild or moderate depression. With this increasing use of medication (there are around 14,000 licensed medicines in the UK – that's a lot!) you hear of some medicines being in short supply these days – with patients receiving these medications having to shop around between pharmacies sometimes, or even go back to their GP to get a different prescription for an alternative drug.

One problem for the older generation in particular is the increasing switch to online ordering of prescribed medication; and some GPs declining to accept telephone requests for repeat prescriptions. This is very hard for an elderly person living a long way from their family, in an area where there is limited broadband and they do not have access to a computer or smartphone, or maybe have a disability such as chronic arthritis or early dementia, that may limit their dexterity to use a tech device.

Community pharmacies are still very much valued by their local population – for their ease of access for most people and the speed of the service and the availability of on-site pharmacists. A new service, Pharmacy First, for which pharmacies in England can be paid £1,000 per month for its provision, is being piloted just now whereby a person can go directly to a pharmacy rather than a GP for the next supply of their contraceptive pill (by being referred or signposted by their GP or sexual health clinic), or to get treatment that includes antibiotics if they have one or more of seven common minor conditions: earache, impetigo, sinusitis, sore throat, shingles, infected insect bite, or an uncomplicated urinary tract infection in women. This will hopefully then free up more GP capacity in local general practices (even as many as 10 million GP appointments per year – very politically hopeful!!), just as it has done by pharmacists administering the seasonal influenza vaccine – where nearly five million 'flu vaccines were provided by community pharmacies in England last winter. The growing proportion of pharmacists who are independent prescribers helps too, as they can initiate and sign off medications that otherwise would need managing by an overseeing GP.

Hopefully the increasing interest in, and extension of community pharmacies' services will help to preserve them as viable businesses – as many pharmacies report unprecedented operational challenges and financial worries these days, with shortages of pharmacists and other staff, and increasing numbers of requests for healthcare advice from members of the public. The number of vacancies for pharmacists in England is around 16%, and around 20% of vacancies for pharmacy technicians who work alongside them, in the various teams. A recent report from the House of Commons and another from the National Pharmacy Association, described community pharmacy funding as having fallen by a third in the last ten years; and that more than 1,400 community pharmacies have closed in the last seven years, with 400 or so of these closing in the last year. There still seems to be good access though, with nine out of ten of the population in England being less than a 20-minute walk from their nearest local pharmacy.

Nowadays more community pharmacists are employed in groups of general practices by their overseeing Primary Care Networks in an umbrella arrangement, with recent funding by the government in

England. They play an increasing role in promoting people's self-care and preventing their ill-health, especially for those with long-term health conditions. Some have chosen to be employed directly. They are a great help for medication reviews, especially where over the years, some people have gradually been prescribed five or more medications as they develop new conditions and these need to be considered together as some prescribed medicines might not fit with others – what's called 'polypharmacy'. I was chatting to Ian the other day, who's aged 75 years old. He told me that he'd been taking six lots of medication since he had a heart attack 20 years ago and had not had any follow up reviews by a heart specialist in the local hospital, so his GPs had just kept them as repeat prescriptions and renewed them every year by rote. He's not at all sure that he still needs them all!

One confusing term that's being used more and more in the provision of NHS care, is 'social prescriber' who tend to be described as 'link workers' too. These are not prescribers of medication, but staff employed to provide help and promote healthy lifestyles for patients with anxiety, and those at an early stage of developing other health problems such as pre-diabetes. So, enabling people to use the services available to them in their local community to improve their wellbeing, or clear their debt, find a job or accommodation.

Chapter 8. Obesity – a huge problem!

Obesity occurs when a person's energy intake well exceeds their energy output, from eating too much and undertaking too little physical activity. The outcome is greatly influenced by their genetic predisposition, behavioural patterns and cultural influences. It's thought that a person's genes may contribute to 25-70% of the variation in adiposity between different people. Genes may affect the metabolism of food, fat storage, and eating behaviour, such as underactivity or overeating. But there are many other causes of obesity too, such as metabolic disorders like an underactive thyroid, or taking medication like steroids, or pressures from sleep disorders or social deprivation. Some people with low self-esteem may consume too much food that's high in sugar and fat – as part of their comfort eating; or be more likely to have eating disorders, such as bulimia or depression.

The puzzle about the relationship between the genetics and size of a person's adipose (fat) cells was what lured me into medical research in the first place. When I was a third-year medical student at Nottingham University in 1973, a hospital consultant enrolled me into helping with a project that he wanted to do – to find out if the size of a person's fat cells was linked to their obese category. He'd already designed the method – and in those days there was nowhere to submit your research protocol for medical ethics approval, and no need to get patient consent to deliver what you wanted to do to them – no national 'rules' as far as I knew. This Dr Andrew could just do what he wanted, or told me to do for him, to the 20 'fat' patients he had selected. So, using a lung biopsy kit – which was like a sizeable syringe with a large pointed tube, I just plunged it into the patient's abdomen to suck out fat samples – from memory, the chunk of fat extracted was about one inch long, in size. This was then bottled up with the patient's name, age and any other relevant medical details and sent to a laboratory, where Dr Andrew had arranged for the technician to analyse the size and content of the fat cells, in these samples of adipose tissues. When one of the 20 patients refused to let me plunge the biopsy needle into their tummy and walked off, I was one sample short. So, I just asked a medical student friend if I could get a sample of fat from his tummy – so that I'd please the consultant and not let him down. This was pretty painful and took some doing as Dave was not fat – maybe slightly plump - and so he did not have much fat to delve into.

The consultant was very pleased that he'd successfully delegated the biopsy taking to me (whilst he sat reading the paper elsewhere in the doctors' mess with a cup of tea probably). I was relieved that I had not punctured anyone's intestine in error (especially my friend Dave's) and just sucked fat samples out. The laboratory staff analysed the fat cells and found that most of them were on the large size – which Dr Andrew thought would be the case – concluding that they had been born to be obese and so it was not their fault that they were. I did actually win First prize in the British Medical Association student research competition later that year for my work: Campbell R (my maiden name).
An investigation of a method for the determination of the type of cellularity of adipose tissue in obese subjects.

I've just looked up the research literature on this subject to see that there is still some uncertainty about the effects of fat cell size. The systematic review that I found was published in 2022, 49 years after my own research as a student; it found 2,348 publications on the subject and analysed 154 research papers in depth. They found that fat cell size predicts numerous obesity-related complications such as lipid dysmetabolism, ectopic fat accumulation, insulin resistance and cardiovascular disorders. It looks like we were ahead of our time in doing that research nearly 50 years ago – but I just hope that none of the patients I plunged the biopsy suction syringe into suffered too many after effects. We were invited to present on the research soon afterwards, at an important event with more than a hundred doctors in the audience. Dr Andrew wanted to take all the credit, so I just sat and listened to him bragging about the project, and resolved to do any future research in a much more sensible and thoughtful way, taking into account patients' perspectives and their safety.

As I started out at Medical School I became more aware of the effects of health inequalities on people's wellbeing. That linked with my initial research interest in obesity. I realised that being breast fed conferred benefits on an infant's well-being compared with bottle feeding, that more mothers in lower social class groups bottle fed compared with those in the higher social class groups, and that the presence of obesity in an infant who is one year old might be linked with bottle feeding. I published my take on this research in THE BRITISH NUTRITION FOUNDATION bulletin in 1975, which was a real accolade for a medical student in those days.

After publishing a book on *Obesity and Overweight Matters in Primary Care* in 2001, I started to get better known as an expert on the subject (self-invented – I just wrote about it in a seemingly knowledgeable way!). That led to me being invited to join as a member of the Royal College of Physicians' Obesity Working Group between 2008-2012 representing GPs, and presenting on *Lifestyle Support Programme services* at the national Royal College of General Practitioners' Obesity Conference in London, in 2012, and at an international conference in Amsterdam. Alongside these commitments, writing and talking, I led on creating a free to use, lifestyle support programme for the local population in Stoke-on-Trent in 2010 with Dr Zafar, a public health colleague, to which local general practice teams could direct overweight patients. It ran for many years and motivated lots of ordinary people to change their behaviour – taking regular exercise, using local gyms which were freely available to people who couldn't otherwise have afforded the costs, and promoting healthy eating and other sensible lifestyle habits.

Over the years my long-suffering husband Chris has got used to being a guinea pig for some of my ideas, and has helped me in practical ways. On one occasion he dressed up in a 'fat suit' that we rented, and stood beside me on the speakers' platform to mimic a typical obese patient, to a conference audience of doctors and nurses. We were showcasing how their overweight patients could be prescribed exercise and motivated to make lifestyle changes with the local lifestyle support scheme – and what a difference that could make to their everyday lives and appearance six months later, say. When Chris went off behind the scenes, stepped out of the fat suit and then returned as a slimmed down version – it made a great impact on the audience who'd all been taken in by the 'fat suit' persona. Many knew he was my husband and just thought he'd gained an awful lot of weight recently (through comfort eating – maybe as a result of living with me?)!

I was invited to become a member of the National Institute for Health and Care Excellence (NICE) committee in 2013-14, that was evolving national guidelines on overweight and obesity in adults. Oh dear! I was only the only doctor on the committee, a few others were patients, some were representing commercial businesses like Weight Watchers, there was a psychologist, an analyst and others. We had three in-person meetings in London at NICE headquarters every couple of months; we were not paid and were expected to do a lot of reading of reports and so on before meetings. To start with I enjoyed the challenge and interactions with committee members. But soon I became more and more aware of the stigma that they were chucking at me, from my using the term 'obese' in my contributions to the committee when giving a doctor's perspective. I had experienced that in my GP consultations too in a different context. I always felt that I needed to help my patient to understand that by being obese they were creating other health problems for themselves, like developing diabetes or cancers that they wouldn't have had otherwise, or having a low mood created by their poor self-esteem or self-efficacy which then took them on a cycle of overeating and sitting around. But I'd found that by their GP being honest with them, that could trigger change and nearly every patient would then go on to make an appointment with one of our practice nurses to start out on a supported weight loss programme. I finished my term on the NICE committee and the guidelines were updated and published soon afterwards. But when I applied to be a member of a NICE committee several years later and was asked at interview about my previous experience, I was put in the 'NICE do not want to include you on any terms' box, just because I'd emphasised at my interview that it was important to have an independent medical perspective on the guidance committee, even if that did not fit with what members of the public or representatives of organisations with their own biases, wanted to hear. NICE does seem still to be in the thralls of organisations that have budgets to spend; looking at their online advert for their annual conference in 2025, they are relaying with a colourful chart the backgrounds of the people who attended their national conference in 2023, ranging from 4% having 'direct control or influence' over more than £20million, and 32% having such control over more than a £1million budget; implying that there may be business opportunities for delegates who attend their next conference presumably.

In 2012, I was often shocked to discover how little fellow GPs, nurses and other primary care staff seemed to know about what healthy eating meant, what reliable advice they should be giving their patients about the number of calories they should be eating (or drinking) per day based upon their age, gender and current weight, and how that matched portion sizes of food containing fat, carbohydrates, protein etc. So, I devised a questionnaire with a GP friend and we aimed to determine how accurately health professionals would estimate the calorie content of a range of food and drink products and the calorie equivalence in physical activity for a man or woman of normal weight, and those who are obese. We had 145 responses from the doctors and nurses we surveyed, with an 86% response rate and found that the nature and extent of exercise required to burn off commonly consumed foods, drinks and snacks remained a mystery to many respondents who were mainly working as clinicians on the frontline, with close contact with patients!

At the time national NICE guidelines for England recommended a daily diet that contained 600kcal/day fewer calories than that required for weight maintenance, for someone to achieve a reasonable weight loss over many months. It looked like health professionals then were not very well informed as to how to help their patients to tackle the obesity epidemic and associated diseases, with a particular focus on knowing and calculating calorie requirements, calorie content of foods and appropriate portion sizes, and exercise requirements for individual patients. We published the article in the Nursing Standard newspaper and got a lot of good feedback. But there were also some negative remarks and concerns from health professionals – how initiating discussions with a patient when you notice that they are obese and they don't seem to be concerned about their body shape, can be challenging and sometimes perceived by the patient as being offensive.

Nowadays, the calorie content of foods and drinks is clearly declared on packaging, so hopefully the public are more aware of what exactly they are consuming; but I still think most people (including health professionals) are pretty ignorant about how many calories they can work off by walking say 10,000 steps, and how that varies according to their weight and gender, their speed of walking and if their activity is uphill or downhill for most of the way. Some smartwatches do well in monitoring the extent and vigour of physical activity – but that also emphasises the health inequalities that are exacerbated by deprivation and the ensuing digital divide between the well off and the poor, who can't afford such digital aids.

And now?

The number of people who can be classed as obese across the world has nearly tripled since 1975! Since 1980 the proportion of the UK population who are thought to be either overweight, or obese, has almost doubled from 36% to 63%. In 1980, 6% of men and 8% of women in the UK were considered to be obese. By 1995, rates had risen so that 14% of men and 17% of women were thought to be obese; now it's estimated that 27% of men and 29% of women are obese, which equates to more than 12 million people in the UK. In addition though, 41% more men are classed as overweight (but not obese) compared to 31% more women who are considered to be overweight too. If the numbers of people who are obese continue to increase, then Cancer Research UK has estimated that by 2040, more than 21 million adults in the UK will be obese. This undue weight gain starts in childhood for many, with one fifth of children aged under five years old who are living in England being thought to be overweight or obese nowadays; with a quarter having tooth decay- presumably linked to eating lots of sugary foods and drinks.

Statistics vary according to the levels of deprivation, so in the most deprived areas in England (such as Stoke-on-Trent where I practised as a GP for around 20 years), around 39% of women are living with obesity, compared with 22% in the least deprived areas (the comparative data for men is 30% in the most deprived areas versus 22% in the least deprived areas). It's affecting all age groups too – 38% of 10-11 year olds in England are now thought to be overweight or obese, giving them a higher risk of developing diabetes.

Obesity is still one of the top five causes of premature death in the UK – as well as high blood pressure, alcohol and drug use and smoking. It is classed as a medical condition associated with excessive fat deposition in the body. It is diagnosed when someone's BMI (basal metabolic index) is greater than 30kg/m^2. But try to remember that obesity is a clinical description with associated health implications, and not a judgement on someone's appearance!

BMI is a simple index of weight-for-height that is used to classify how overweight someone is, and to estimate their adiposity (proportion of fat in their body) as a rough guide. The same measure is used for both sexes and all ages of adults. People who have a high level of muscle mass (usually young men) may incorrectly be placed in the 'overweight' category, so any BMI measure must be interpreted with caution. People with an Asian ethnicity appear to suffer health consequences if they've a lower BMI than Caucasians do. A BMI of 23kg/m^2 and above is classed as being overweight for south Asians living in the UK, as opposed to a BMI of 25kg/m^2 and above for Caucasians.

Moderate to extreme obesity can shorten a person's life expectancy by 3-10 years due to the associated health condition(s) that they usually develop alongside. A person with a raised BMI has a higher risk of developing health conditions such as heart disease, musculoskeletal disorders and some cancers. Being obese for instance, gives someone around an 85% chance of developing type 2 diabetes, that they would not have had if they had remained at an ideal weight. The numbers of younger people with type 2 diabetes is shooting up – recent NHS figures reveal that about 168,000 of people under the age of 40 years who live in England have this condition already, which is around 40% more than ten years ago; the popularity of junk food these days has very much contributed to this evolving health crisis. Obesity is associated with infertility and miscarriage too. And in later life, people who are obese are more likely to have a stroke or a cardiovascular event like a heart attack, or have high blood pressure.

The NHS costs associated with obesity are estimated to be about £19 billion per year in the UK, taking into account the consequences of obesity due to the many associated health conditions and complications. The number of people in England who are admitted for hospital care where their obesity is a factor, is around one in fifty adults per year. The draw of eating highly processed foods that reduce a person's satiety increases their calorie intake as they eat more as a norm. So, the government needs to scale up public health led, preventative services and practicable interventions for people of all ages, to motivate and support those who are overweight to eat more healthily and overcome their physical inactivity at all stages of their life, which will improve their mental health too.

A recent King's Fund briefing reported that in 2019/20, there were more than one million hospital admissions in England linked to patients with obesity. These admissions were three times more likely to relate to people from the most deprived areas, compared to the least deprived areas. Women accounted for around two-thirds of hospital admissions where obesity was logged as a factor. We need a widescale public health approach that focuses in the main on prevention as well as treatment and takes into account the wider determinants of health, to minimise health inequalities. We must find ways to engage the population at large, and empower individuals to care for themselves, to reduce pressures on the NHS and care services that could be avoided if more people lived healthier lives. There are popular well known behavioural approaches highlighted in health magazines and the general press, such as intermittent fasting, high protein and low carbohydrate consumption, small energy deficits – often associated with the celebrities who advocate them.

Despite these excessive NHS costs and the linked wider economic impact of obesity due to loss of productivity, absence from work and premature mortality, recent research has found that obesity is actually not a current priority for 37 of the 42 Integrated Care Boards across England. So, the postcode lottery still exists, for access to NHS costed obesity related treatment.

There is more of a focus on prevention these days with testing for people with pre-diabetes being offered at scale to adults in the UK. A recent National Diabetes Audit found that nearly four million people in England are thought to be at risk of developing diabetes type 2 and are classed as being pre-diabetic (my husband Chris is one of those – and being labelled as pre-diabetic has influenced his dietary choices, so that he eats less carbohydrates – most days anyway!).

I've always had a passion to empower people to self-care for themselves better. One way that I have tried to help people with their weight management has been by making them more aware of how a range of digital aids might help them, like accessing apps and trustworthy websites to engage with others, or read relevant and reliable information. A real winner was a book I co-authored on using digital aids informing the reader about how they could be smart with their weight using a range of digital routes – like the Couch to 5K app which is aimed at those who don't regularly exercise or keep active, to make a start. That app has been such a hit nationally that it apparently had more than five million downloads by mid-2021; it was seen as reliable as it is recommended by Public Health England – and it is free.

The NHS Digital Weight Management programme was launched in England in 2021, providing free online support for people who are ready to tackle their being overweight, and adopt healthier lifestyles. It is a 12-week online behavioural and lifestyle programme that people can access with their smartphone or tablet or computer with internet access, after being referred by their GP or a pharmacist. They must be 18 years old or older, have a BMI greater than 30 (a little lower for people from black, Asian, and ethnic minority backgrounds) and must also have diabetes, high blood pressure, or both. There are lots of good stories as to how well people have done in losing weight with this online programme – so long as they are motivated to keep going with it for at least three months.

Another great success for me was leading a local NHS based technology enabled care team initially, to focus on older people with diabetes and set them up with an Alexa Echo Show, along with some reliable digital weighing scales that calculated their BMI too. The messages and information relayed by their Alexa kits really did help with their weight management, and about half of those who needed to had lost significant excess weight in the first three months of trying the Echo Show out.

So many people have sedentary lifestyles these days – if they have a desk job or watch too much television or are on their phone screen non-stop. I led on a community-type project recently designing and giving out hundreds of 'My Health Kits' to local people, one of which focussed on helping them with their weight management. We talked to people who knew they were eating fast foods that are too high in sugar and fat, with too large portion sizes. They often described that other members of their family had poor dietary habits too; and we realised that healthy foods are up to three times more expensive on a calorie-for-calorie basis, than junk foods.

There tend to be more fast-food retail outlets in areas with the worst deprivation like Stoke-on-Trent where this programme was focused.

The feedback we got from individual recipients about the weight management kits that contained digital weighing scales, the 'Smart with your Weight' book, elastic exercise bands, and portion plate was fantastic – like these:

"I had been to my doctor recently and he said that all the problems that I was complaining of were related to my being overweight (anxiety, depression, sleeping issues, blood pressure). I have started to make healthier diet changes by cutting down on rice intake and chapatis. I'm getting there!"

"I have used the weight loss book provided in the kit. 'Smart with your weight'. This book is really clear and offers information in a non-preachy manner with lots of little suggestions."

"Some weight loss advice is an all or nothing approach whereas this book offers advice that is achievable and makes you feel weight loss can be achieved by lots of small steps."

"I am aware that I'm overweight, and this kit has helped to give me the motivation to start looking at my lifestyle. Over the past 15 years I have been advised to lose weight at my GP surgery. I have been offered medication to help me lose weight five times, but that medication would not have been feasible for me."

Many hospitals across the UK have made substantial investments in the staff and equipment to undertake bariatric surgery. This weight reduction surgery is offered each year to a tiny minority of patients who are obese (that is, their BMI is more than 40kg/m^2; or at lower thresholds depending on their ethnicity, or if they have a significant health condition such as poorly managed type 2 diabetes or heart disease that could be very much improved if they lost weight), once all other acceptable treatment options have been exhausted; usually as a last resort. The cost of bariatric surgical treatment is similar to, or less than, a year's worth of medication for those patients with morbid obesity. So that's a massive saving for the health economy, as most patients who have bariatric surgery go on to reduce or stop using medication for several health conditions associated with their former obesity, such as diabetes, hypertension, obstructive sleep apnoea and so on. And over time, they will need to use the NHS less and less as their health and wellbeing improves. My problem as a GP was that although I was supportive of a person who would benefit from having bariatric surgery, it was easy for them to get lost to follow-up after their surgery, as so many dropped out of sight and didn't get the long-term follow on blood tests and nutritional supplements that they required – from a community dietitian, pharmacist and/or general practice team. So, a shared-care model is needed to underpin a local care pathway as a norm across the NHS, following on after all substantive hospital care, and not just for complicated cases like post-bariatric surgery.

Unfortunately, over the last ten years or so obesity management has been shifted from general practice to more complex settings and tiers of care. New clinical treatments for weight loss are skyrocketing, as people search online and initiate their own treatment – like arranging to have weight loss surgery abroad, in countries like Turkey. Injectable weight loss drugs like semaglutide (manufactured under various brand names) have been used to treat diabetes for more than a decade and are now being used for redressing obesity too, by reducing a person's appetite, making them feel fuller as well as increasing their insulin levels and thus blood glucose. This drug is given as a weekly self-administered injection into a person's thigh, abdomen or upper arm, and has had a lot of public press recently promoting its effectiveness for weight loss (and costs up to £1,500 per patient per annum), when used alongside a reduced calorie diet and enhanced exercise plan. Tirzepatide is another weight loss medication requiring a weekly injection too, that's been recently launched with the hope that those using it will lose up to 20% of their weight – so this is an expanding market, and maybe such competition in the pharmaceutical industry will drive down costs. There are very many adverts by online pharmacies who claim that they can arrange next day delivery of such medication in the UK. It's not clear how they check that the person ordering online really does fit the national prescribing guidelines to ensure that such medicines are used safely and effectively, and not abused in some way – for example, by the person ordering the medication giving a fictional account that their body mass index is sky high and they have pre-diabetes (which they've never been tested for). So self-initiated obesity treatments like these can put a person at risk and are unsafe – if the treatment was not justified and there is no follow on after-care to spot side effects like mood disorders, constipation, headaches and more with this medication; or possible wound infection and bowel obstruction from gastric bypass surgery.

But just to add, out of the blue NICE has just invited me personally to join a Scientific Advice Project providing advice on obesity; so they do value my expertise, which is great news.

Chapter 9. Prison healthcare

How it was

By the mid-1990s, when I'd been working as a doctor for 20 years I was interested in how healthcare was provided in prisons, after seeing some patients who were newly out of prison at my general practice, who seemed to be mental health wrecks. So, I offered to extend the quality improvement healthcare programme that I was leading on for the population served by general practices in Staffordshire, and review what was on offer healthcare wise in our local prisons. I wanted to share our learning about the good parts and gaps in the quality of care being provided in local general practices with prison doctors, and hopefully learn from them some great lessons that we could adopt in general practice. I got permission to go into all six prisons in Staffordshire from each prison governor. Oh dear! What a learning experience that was for me – just comparing the quality of health care provided to the patients registered with a typical general practice, versus the measly care available to a prison inmate. Though I wasn't too surprised as my interest had been stoked by a couple of ex-prisoners coming to consult me with varying ailments and realising that they'd had very limited healthcare whilst staying in prison and needed urgent treatments from a GP and local hospital, for their prevailing physical and mental ill-health.

The six Staffordshire based prisons were very different from each other. One was for young offenders and the other five varied as to whether they were high security or of a lower level, and one of these prisons was just for female prisoners. I got used to going into each prison through the public entrance and being checked. Then meeting the prison healthcare staff and relaxedly interviewing some of the prisoners individually to get their perspectives too, on a one-to-one basis in a public room.
(I rewarded each of them with a mars bar having taken a big bag of them openly through prison security. These were banned by the governor in the Category C high security prison because he thought that they might initiate a stampede of prisoners grabbing them from me – so I ended up with more than 50 mars bars stashed away in a cupboard at home. Instead of triggering the stampede envisaged by the prison governor it was my young kids instead who took the opportunity to grab some and

gorge on them before their parents realised that they'd helped themselves!!!).

Only two of the prisons had a qualified doctor on site (for part of the day anyway) – the rest had visiting local GPs whom the prison paid to come in to provide a half day of patient consultations once or twice a week. The prison officers taking responsibility for healthcare had a month's training on top of their usual role, as I understood it – similar to a healthcare assistant in today's NHS with limited clinical experience and basic skills.

Healthcare in prisons was via private providers in the 1990s – it was not the responsibility of an NHS provider until the early 2000s. Until June 1999, doctors recruited to work in prisons were required only to be 'registered medical practitioners' rather than having appropriate specialist training in prison healthcare.

Prisons seemed to buy in medication then in the same way that they bought in food for the inmates. Rob who was a prisoner in the 1990s knew of a guy who had stomach problems – he developed a stomach ulcer and his symptoms got worse. He had read in a newspaper about an experimental medication and requested it from the doctor visiting the prison. The prison bought it in for him, privately. His prison invested in this medication as they could not shift that prisoner on to another prison (as they did routinely) until he was a bit better and the bleeding from his anus had stopped. They bought him the high calorie drinks that he requested too. He started to improve and was moved on to another prison; so Rob never saw him again and they lost touch.

Rob saw the prison doctor or nurse weekly too – as he also had digestive problems. There was no confidentiality – he was seen in an office with other prison staff walking in and out, earwigging if they wanted to. The nurse agreed to Rob's request that he could be prescribed gluten-free food; it was much more expensive and it was exclusive to Rob who then got his own big box of rice crispies at breakfast, instead of competing with other prisoners who were usually scrabbling for a share of basic cereals. There was no evidence that he needed gluten-free food – he just wanted his own supply of much tastier food. But the nurse had confirmed that he should have it and so the prison (and each successive one he was transferred to thereafter) bought him a range of gluten-free foods, and he remembers fondly having his very own tasty cakes that no other prisoner could snatch.

What I remember specifically in the early-1990s in these six prisons was the lack of opportunity for a prisoner to have a confidential consultation between them and a doctor. The prison etiquette was to distrust any prisoner and for the doctor to fear being attacked or robbed of their possessions. I saw that there was always a prison guard sitting or standing in the consulting room, listening to the prisoner/doctor conversation. What prisoner would have dared to share their personal insights about their mental health or how they were being bullied by others or humiliated with the prison staff listening in? They knew that sharing confidential matters could lead to some pay back from other prisoners, or even the prison guards themselves.

In those days it seemed to be all about preserving safety from the prison service perspective and not about providing personalised health care for each prisoner. For example, in the young male offenders' prison that I visited, those with asthma shared the same inhaler that was kept in the pocket of the prison guard nominated as the healthcare lead on that shift, who would take it to the cell of the prisoner who was calling out that they needed it to help with their breathing – to take a puff from it. The prison healthcare team explained to me when I looked appalled at this arrangement that this was to avoid mayhem across the prison cells and shared space. If each prisoner who said they had asthma had their own inhaler in their pocket, they'd soon be sharing it, enabling other prisoners to take a puff or two or many…and creating highs for the person using it from the inhaler medication. They didn't have enough healthcare prison guards to go to the treatment room and fetch and carry a separate inhaler dedicated to an individual prisoner for whom it was prescribed, so that was why the healthcare officer carried the jointly-shared inhaler, to have on standby.

This non-caring approach to overseeing the use of a shared inhaler fitted in with all the other prisons' etiquette for doling out medication prescribed for prisoners. When Ann gave out daily prescribed drugs in the late 1990s in her prison nurse role, when having fully trained healthcare staff in post had become the norm, she was based in a side room with a hatch that opened into the corridor. Everyone queued up for their prescribed medication or ad hoc paracetamol – in the morning and early evening, at set times. Ann watched each of them put the tablets or medicine she gave them in their mouths and she inspected that they had swallowed their medication and that there were no drugs on their tongue (to be able to pass on to another person later) before they moved on! Prisoners could not store paracetamol for their own use in their pocket or cell for when they needed it - they always had to request it. So basic access to medicine was a barrier – an adult prisoner who was in pain could not access paracetamol easily. It doesn't make any sense to an outsider used to being able to buy over the counter medicines as, and when, needed – but then the prison had to prioritise the preservation of prisoners' safety, where prison staff availability was very constrained!

I did share my findings and perspectives about the quality of the provision of prison health care with each governor of the six prisons that I visited, and how they could consider adopting clinical audit as an approach to improve the healthcare services on offer in their prison. This was about the access and availability of care, as much as about the quality of care provided. For instance, this should be about taking a more proactive approach for prisoners with long-term conditions like asthma and diabetes, and trying to put better treatments in place to prevent the deterioration of their long-term health conditions and enhance their mental wellbeing. Some of the prison governors listened even though I was an outsider, however well intentioned. And I was even invited to Styal prison in Cheshire the following year to share my clinical insights and suggestions for them to consider pushing for quality improvement options there too.

Talking to ex-prisoners who came to see me as a GP in my surgery once they were released, I realised that my experience of the inadequate healthcare provided in these local prisons was typical of prisons across the UK. Alan told me that when he was in a prison in South West England in the 1990s, he heard a guy, Tony, banging on his cell door about 30 yards or so down the corridor at about 10pm – after all the prisoners had retreated to their cells for the night. He was alone in his cell as he was deemed high risk. He kept shouting for help for the next two to three hours, but prison officers did not look inside the cell to view or talk to him – they just thought he was messing about and trying to play them and get their attention. Alan kept hearing the banging/buzzer going on. Then silence – and Tony was found dead and cold the next morning when the prison officers opened up the cell, to realise that he had died around 1am when all had gone quiet. Alan did not know what Tony had died from (but thought he'd cut his wrists as he saw that there was blood smeared round the corridor later on). He was not aware of any prison officers ('the screws') being suspended or losing their job due to their neglect of their prisoner, Tony.

A friend of mine, Sue, who is a practising nurse was telling me about working as a nurse in the late 1990s, in a **Category B prison** full-time. As a prison nurse she took blood tests, did health examinations for courts, undertook potential suicide reviews, and gave out medication. Nurse Sue was told not to take a pack of syringes/needles for blood testing into prison cells, but to keep them safely in her pocket; and the numbers of needles were checked in/out as she finished her shifts by a senior prison officer. Sue went into a cell on her own with each prisoner to take a blood test or undertake a health review, but carefully positioned herself near to the panic button, which she could press if needed. Many of the prisoners she looked after were on heavy duty painkillers; she remembers about 50% of them being so. The prison doctors went along with it even though such medication was generally unjustified and not needed for their health issues, because the pills kept the prisoners fairly sedated. She witnessed a prisoner asking for more drugs because of the 'terrible pain' they were having; and when the visiting GP refused, Adam the prisoner said: 'I know where your wife and daughters live' as a threat to compel the doctor to prescribe more. Sue was a chaperone nurse in that case; with a prison officer standing outside the medical treatment room, rather than inside it as it would have been in the 1970s; and she watched the prison doctor flinch, but be brave, and not give in to the prisoner's outrageous demands.

And now?
Prison health care was omitted from that provided by the NHS at its establishment in 1948. Responsibility was transferred to the NHS from the Prison Medical Service in 2006. The NHS primary care trusts then became responsible for commissioning and providing health services to prisoners in their areas, including emergency care and ambulance services. The Health and Social Care Act that was passed in 2012 triggered more changes to the commissioning of prison healthcare in England, including providing dental care. So now, healthcare within prisons is delivered by both NHS providers and independent operators who have been commissioned, such as the Practice Plus Group that provides primary and nursing care, sexual health, mental health and substance misuse services. The Care Quality Commission does inspect prison healthcare and social care services now as an independent national regulator.

The doctor who chairs the British Medical Association's Forensic and Secure Environment Committee (Dr MB) recently gave me some great insights into how well (or not) prison healthcare is working these days. He's been working in secure hospitals and prisons since 1996, and has seen great improvements in forensic care over the last 30 years. He believes that the shift of responsibility for prison healthcare from the Home Office to the Department of Health has made a real difference, so that good quality NHS care is the norm now across UK prisons; although the provision of healthcare for some in police custody and immigration facilities remains outside the responsibility of the NHS for its 'on the ground' delivery. There is much better integration between community primary care and prison healthcare through improved data sharing; though the lack of medication reconciliation in, and out of, prison is still a key issue so that prisoners who are newly confined, or discharged, may go for weeks without their ongoing prescribed drugs. This issue can be exacerbated if the prisoner or person detained in custody has poor English language skills; so easy access to interpreters in person or by phone is essential.

A real challenge these days is providing accessible mental health services. Around half of all prisoners in England are thought to have a mental health problem, so rates of self-harm and drug addiction in the prison population are really high. NHS England provides a Liaison and Diversion service which aims to improve health outcomes for those in contact with the justice system by ensuring that effective early assessments are made of vulnerable people in custody, so that they can refer the prisoner as appropriate for the specialised medical treatment and support that they need. The Royal College of Psychiatrists estimates that around 10% of the prison population (more than 8,000 people a year in England), should be diverted to receive mental health treatment by the Courts, rather than be kept in custody where their conditions worsen. This is especially important for those prisoners with learning disabilities or difficulties who are almost three times as likely as other inmates to have clinically significant anxiety or depression.

Between June 2020 and June 2021 there were 3,808 incidents of self-harm per 1,000 female prisoners compared to 546 per 1,000 male prisoners. And put that in the context of there being around 98,000 people in prison in England, Wales, Northern Ireland and Scotland now according to recent national statistics – far more than in 1990 when there were just under 45,000 prisoners on average – and that increase has made overcrowding in prisons much worse. About 11,000 people who are under 25 years of age are in young offender institutions and prisons in England and Wales. About 4% of the prison population are women.
The length of sentences is currently under review with a government edict to free up more spaces in prisons for those in custody waiting for the Court's decision on their cases. Nearly one-fifth of the prison population are over 50 years old, and many have chronic illness(es) and poor mental health and/or a physical disability; with a past history of alcohol and/or substance misuse. Of course, that means that prison buildings and cells need to be adjusted to accommodate older people with poor mobility and who lack independence – another challenge!

It takes a lot of manpower too to take a prisoner to hospital or another external healthcare site when it needs a couple of prison escort staff to accompany them, using restraints as necessary. Prisoners find it a real stigma to be seen in a public setting like a hospital waiting room wearing handcuffs, too. And the accompanying prison officer will generally sit in a hospital clinic room with the prisoner, so that the doctor or nurse feels safe – thus breaching patient confidentiality and making the prisoner uncomfortable in disclosing how they are feeling. There just isn't that spare capacity amongst prison staff for this to be an easy arrangement and thus fewer prisoners access hospital services, than do the general population; with a lot of non-attendances at booked hospital outpatient clinics. Remote healthcare set up between the prison and clinician in their own base is increasingly common now; evolving from the 2% or so of outpatient consultations for prisoners in 2017/18 that were carried out as phone or video consultations.

It does look though as if prison staff have a low threshold for making a 999 call for help, as three in four of the emergency calls they make for an ambulance are considered inappropriate, compared to the national average for the general population being one in eight calls. Sometimes calls get cancelled before the ambulance reaches the prison to pick up the prisoner; and just 19% of prisoners are judged as needing to be taken to hospital when the ambulance does arrive, which compares with 51% for their usual pickup response rate.

There are a considerable number of deaths in custody – for example, in the 12 months to December 2023 there were 93 self-inflicted deaths in custody, a 22% increase from the previous year; many happen in the first few weeks that the prisoner is in custody. The rate of self-harm was high during this period – with 805 incidents per 1000 prisoners! The rate of self-harm in female prisons is much higher than that in male establishments; but only 3% of all deaths in custody were female prisoners.

There's often a hotchpotch of care where there's a lack of communication between the previous GP or community health care provider, and the prison healthcare system. So, potential errors can include stopping medication that had previously been prescribed in the community, for a newly admitted prisoner or giving them incorrect treatment - dose or type of medication. In one case, when a patient re-registered at my GP practice after being released from custody in 2015, there was no record of them having been away from home (in prison) and no records from any other health provider. If Bob hadn't told me he'd just been released from prison and described his health and wellbeing issues, I'd have thought he'd just not bothered coming to our practice to see a doctor or nurse for the last three years. His diabetes was way out of control as he'd not been taking any tablets for weeks, since he'd been discharged from prison. He said he'd been diagnosed as having diabetes whilst in prison and did take some tablets regularly then to control his blood sugar levels.

There are so many reports of this lack of continuity between the outside world and prison healthcare that I've heard from listening to other doctors and ex-prisoners about their experiences recently:

- Gladys was not given her medication for her attention deficit hyperactivity disorder (ADHD) that she was on when she lived at home, when she went into prison for several days. Her mental health really deteriorated and she only just got by with having a really low mood, improving when her treatment was restarted.
- Dan wasn't so lucky. It took the prison healthcare team eight days to get him his mental health medication after he was convicted. When they finally gave him his medication, his mental health had deteriorated so much that he had developed severe paranoia, from which he never completely recovered. And when he did eventually get his medication it was twice a day at 9am and 4pm as medicines were distributed to meet regime/staffing requirements, as opposed to patients' needs. Getting his second dose so early meant that Dan was then drowsy all evening and then awake during the night from 3am – whereas if he'd taken his second daily dose at 9pm, he'd have been in bed asleep when the drowsy effect took place.
- Liam was even worse. He was clearly experiencing hallucinations and delusions, and had not left his cell or washed for several weeks. Prison officers thought that he was 'acting up' to stay in his single cell and do what he wanted. So, they had not called for a specialist mental health review. When Liam eventually had an in-depth mental health assessment, he started to improve once on the new medication – but this was a period of his life that he can still remember and impacts on him and how he's feeling now, even a year later.

People have suggested that each prisoner should have a medical passport that they carry with them that logs their health conditions and current medications prescribed, to ensure their continuity of care.

And there's still a real gender issue. In Wales there are six prisons, but none have facilities for female prisoners with severe mental health problems. When such a woman is taken into custody they are transported to a prison in England – and that makes family visits to the female prisoner very difficult. Similarly in Scotland, there is no high security inpatient care for women with mental health issues, and they also get transferred to an English prison for secure inpatient care and detention. It was recognised early in the COVID pandemic that overcrowding of prisoners in confined spaces with minimal ventilation and poorly resourced healthcare was going to exacerbate infection between prisoners, and for prison staff. Reports of the COVID-19 death rates among prisoners in England and Wales in the first year of the pandemic indicated that the death rate from COVID for prisoners was more than three times that of people in the general population, of the same sex and age. That comparatively high death rate from COVID is in keeping too with the high number of natural deaths in prisons. On average prisoners have a life expectancy 20 years lower than that of the general population because of their poor health and wellbeing before, during, and after, being in prison. The average age of someone dying in prison of 'natural causes' is just 67 years old, which is quite a contrast to the average age of death being 81 years old or so for the general population. Many prisoners have a higher risk of heart disease than those in the general population, partly due to their increased likelihood of having had poor lifestyle habits when out in the 'real world', maybe smoking or drinking excess alcohol, unhealthy eating or taking illegal drugs.

A recent Lay Observers' report from volunteers who undertake independent monitoring of people in court custody (and I'm one of them) still highlights this issue – how following a court appearance and a remand in custody or detention order, young people are often retained in their custody cell for several hours whilst appropriate accommodation is sought for them. This prolonged detention may have a negative impact on their mental health and wellbeing. And there doesn't seem to be much progress since I had a similar experience when I was fostering in the 1980s, I got an emergency call from a social worker early one Friday evening. Would we take in Kim aged 16 years old currently in a police cell who had been arrested for stealing goods in a shop? Kim was in a really miserable state and couldn't be sent back to her family home. Her family had come over as asylum seekers on a boat from Vietnam and travelled to England eventually to claim sanctuary – when she was six years old. She became just a normal schoolgirl, wearing makeup and a shortish skirt; but her father brutally assaulted her for her 'westernised' persona and how she dressed. She'd been in custody for 12 hours already so we took her in for the next four weeks whilst her case was sorted.

And there was a recent article in our local paper which included insights from the mother of a teenage boy who was locked up in the young offender prison in Staffordshire that I visited 30 years ago. She described how unsafe the prison is still after hearing horror stories from her son. These related to violent incidents in that prison for the last six months of 2021, with reportedly 82 assaults on prison staff and 105 assaults on the teenage prisoners, with a total of 31 young offenders ending up in hospital! Puts my alarm at the dangers of many young people sharing the same asthma inhaler in that same prison in the 1990s, in perspective!

I was shopping in a retail store recently when a young man came up to me. 'You don't remember me do you doctor??!!' 'Of course I do' I said, playing it safe and not revealing my poor memory for holding patients' detailed medical histories in my brain. I preferred to leave work behind when I exited my general practice to go home at night. 'So, what job do you do now?' I asked him. That led to Carl describing what job he had with a 'I wouldn't be here if it wasn't for you doctor!' And it all came back to me – he'd come out of prison after a three months stretch having taken the rap too for his friends, protecting their identities after being caught stealing from a couple of local shops. Coming out of prison, his family disowned him. I had seen him on his second day out of prison as his GP, and encouraged him to be patient with his family, talk them round and find a job if he could, to get back to a normal life again. So, Carl was telling me when we met up recently, a few years after he'd been released from prison that if it was not for me having been an interested and caring GP he'd have committed suicide in despair at how hostile his family were, and seemingly unforgiving. Now he'd rebuilt his life, still living with his Mum (happily) and holding down a reasonable, stable job in a local store. . . and was back in with his friends too. Great news! But there are wide-reaching effects that imprisonment can have on prisoners and their families, of which we all have to be aware.

Some good news is that a recent inspection at Wormwood Scrubs prison (a Category B prison based in London that holds around 1150 adult men and some young adults) found that all new prisoners had had a health assessment within seven days of arriving at the prison and those who needed to had attended follow up clinics to review the newly arrived inmates with long-term health conditions, like diabetes. And I've just read in the 'Inside Time' newspaper that the charity, Prison Phoenix Trust, is celebrating the healthy positives that have emerged for staff and prisoners in 55 jails across the UK, for those who joined in practising yoga or meditation everyday for a month. So, that's a great way forward for improving prisoners' personal wellbeing at scale.

I went to Styal prison in Cheshire recently - not as an inmate or a doctor, but as a hungry customer to eat in their restaurant, now open to the public! We had great service from some of the current prison inmates who have been recruited to the kitchen and on the restaurant floor, to help prepare them for their daily lives outside prison when they are released, and hopefully be more likely to get a job and get back to a normal life at home.

Dr MB believes that the justice system is a political football. We lock up too many people who have offended due to their drug and alcohol addictions, rather than caring for them appropriately. People could be treated in kinder ways with help from health professionals and with better housing in the community. As in other parts of the NHS, we're short of prison GPs and there isn't a specific training pathway as there is for other specialisms. One solution might be to include opportunities for forensic medicine within the GP training pathway, just as it is for psychiatry specialty training. Then more GPs could have a portfolio career that includes being a GP part-time, alongside being a prison doctor part-time too.

And what about the health and wellbeing of prison staff too these days? A recent survey by the House of Commons Justice Committee found that three quarters of staff who are in direct contact with prisoners don't feel valued for the work they do, and many do not feel safe in their workplaces. Verbal abuse from prisoners is common. But even more alarmingly, about two-thirds of staff report feeling stressed at work, and one in five reported bullying or verbal abuse that they'd received from other prison staff. Seems like there's a workforce crisis in prisons looming too, as well as in the NHS and social care sectors.

Chapter 10. End of life?

I'm not talking about the end of the life of the NHS. No! Let's focus on how and if doctors and nurses can help people under their care to reach a comfortable end, even if it comes as a surprise. The 'end of life' is defined these days as being when people are likely to die within 12 months, and have advanced, progressive, incurable conditions as well as people with life threatening acute conditions who may have only a few hours, days or weeks of life (probably). Palliative care is the relief from pain and other upsetting decline in normal functioning when a person is experiencing advancing, progressive illness. Delivery of such care involves family members too, helping them to cope with their forthcoming bereavement as their loved one deteriorates and nears death. Doctors and nurses are trained to regard a patient at the end of life as a whole person, and not just a tick box exercise.

When Agnes, a 93 year old lady, who had full mental capacity and lived in her own home alone, fell down the stairs recently, she really hurt one of her legs. She wrapped a tea towel round it, but when her care worker Karen arrived for her daily review, she took a peek and could see a bone sticking out near her ankle. Because of the wait for an ambulance, Karen took Agnes to A&E to be seen, and left her there as she needed to get to her next client. The A&E doctor just announced to Agnes in a *not-for-discussion* way that she must have an operation, assuming that as an elderly lady she was not capable of making her own decision, and it would just waste his time to discuss the matter with her. By the time her daughter Marie arrived half an hour later the A&E nurse had already told Agnes she'd be having her operation to 'chop your leg off' later that day. Having Mary on her side, Agnes showed that she still had her faculties and refused to cooperate with having her leg amputated below the knee, as the hospital team instructed. She was admitted to a nursing home instead later that day, where she died happily a few weeks later.
That comfortable, peaceful death was her preference to having a risky operation that would have affected her daily living enormously, if she'd eventually been discharged from the post-operative hospital ward to a nursing home after several weeks – never getting used to trying to move about with only one leg.

Medical and nursing students get to know about the end of life, whilst they are training. My first encounter with a dead body was in my second year as a medical student at Nottingham University. Aged 19 years old I'd never seen a corpse before, let alone touched one. And now we were expected to take turns in groups of six medical students in cutting up a dead body – or 'cadaver' as it was called. Six of us would group round each dissecting table, with the seven naked cadavers laid out respectfully, with some cloth draped over their trunks. The bravest student picked up the scalpel and had a go at cutting through the skin first of all, so that we could extract and feel the body's various organs, such as the kidney, liver, stomach, ovary. Most of the bodies were male which reflected who'd have been the most likely person to gift their body to students to learn from, when they died. It certainly made our anatomy books and the various skeletons (from real humans too) come alive (well not breathing again – just helped us to picture the inside of a human body in real life when patients gave us their medical histories and their symptoms on hospital wards and in other NHS settings). The problem was as students we found touching and carving up dead bodies very upsetting and to mask this some of the students (definitely not me – it was the 'boys') made fun of what we were doing – pinching eyes out of the eye sockets of the cadavers and flicking them at other students grouped round their dissecting tables when the university staff were not looking – being out taking a reprieve from work, or reading in a corner.

But I recently popped into the anatomy suite at Keele University medical school to donate a half-skeleton that a friend still had hanging around their house (actually stored in a box rather than suspended from the ceiling!!), 50 years after they'd bought it as a medical student. In those days bones and skeletons were mainly bought from India via Adam, Rouilly & Co. who described themselves as the 'House for Human Skeletons', but this trade of packs of real human bones came under scrutiny in the UK in the late 1970s, and the exportation ceased in 1985. So now medical students and specialists in training access treasured old boxes of human bones, or plastic replicas; or these days much of this type of teaching is by simulated learning using virtual reality to represent patients lying in beds, or bodies being dismembered, maybe.

I chatted with the anatomy lecturer at Keele University who said that if any medical students were to flick an excised eyeball to another student as a joke these days, they would be immediately suspended from their medical student training, and might well not be reinstated on their university course. What a difference – 50 years on, we are 'dead' respectful of patients' rights, now!

It's really difficult for a doctor or nurse or social carer to have a balanced view about supporting a person to have a comfortable end of life if they've seen a minority of patients actually recover somewhat from a similar illness, even though they had minimal chances of surviving. I know this from my personal experience with my foster son Paul – and here's how..........:

My husband and I did foster a few children for five years early on in my medical career, whilst we were bringing up our own two, then three, children. One boy, Paul aged two years old, had a serious congenital disorder and we knew that when we took him in to live with us that it was for *end of life* care, though we hoped that he would live for many happy years into his twenties.

Tragically Paul died at our home one year later – and I still reflect on how I switched from parent into doctor mode, when I went into his bedroom to check on him, to find that he had collapsed and stopped breathing but was still lovely and warm and of a good colour. I do so wish that I'd left Paul lying there peacefully asleep instead of plunging adrenaline in a syringe into his heart/leaving our own 3 and 5 year old children on their own asleep at home in the middle of the night, to take Paul to hospital. He had a very distressing time in hospital for a week with constant checks by doctors and nurses of his blood pressure and other tests. Luckily the hospital team realised that they couldn't save him and let us take Paul home to die, where he spent two happy weeks gradually deteriorating, but joining in my older son's 6th birthday party where he was fondly wrapped in a blanket smiling and took part in a 'pass the parcel' party game. This sobering experience helped me to learn how others do not accept that a loved one will die soon and try to insist that doctors prescribe whatever treatment might work, whatever the distress it might cause, based on the very slim chance of it working.

With this experience of Paul's last few weeks, I became even more caring of patients at the end of their lives. But it was, and always will be, terribly difficult to certify a young person as dead when you know if things had been different they'd still be alive. Even thirty plus years later I can remember as if it was yesterday certifying two teenagers as dead in their own homes in the same week, **when I was the GP on call for our two practices in Stone.** The first, Sam, was aged 17 years old and I was responding to a call from his father for an emergency visit about 11pm at night (yes, GPs did home visits in the 1990s, day and night!). His father Dan, had popped into Sam's bedroom to say goodnight as he'd been lying up there on his own listening to his radio- which was on at full blast. Dan opened the bedroom door and found Sam lying face down, not breathing and unresponsive. In those days you'd usually phone the GP, not an ambulance, for an emergency visit. So, he phoned our practice and was diverted to my home phone line where I took the call from my lounge sofa 'Sam's not breathing, please help!' I drove quickly and got there carrying my emergency doctor's bag ten minutes later. But there was nothing I could do- he was fairly cold and had been dead for around two hours. It looked like he'd taken bottles of pills and had committed suicide – and that was all confirmed at the post-mortem later on.

The coroner invited me to give evidence at the inquest which I did, supporting his grieving father Dan, whose wife (Sam's Mum) had died from cancer the previous year. This led to long-term support of Dan as you can imagine – with weekly GP appointments for quite some time. Only a few days after certifying Sam's death I was called out to Sian's home by her Mum at 2am. Sian was having a terrible asthma attack triggered by hay fever and had been using her inhalers, but without much improvement and she seemed to have stopped breathing. The family lived out in the middle of the countryside so even though I got up and dressed immediately and drove out a couple of miles down winding country lanes it took me 15 or so minutes to get there. When I arrived, she was lying in the lounge as I ran in with my doctor's bag that stored spare inhalers and a nebuliser too. But I was too late and from what Sian's Mum said with tears pouring down her face, she'd stopped breathing about the time they'd phoned for help. It's still the case that people die from asthma each year in the UK and the more preventive treatment they take via specific inhalers, the better their health and life chances are. Both Sian and Sam had postmortems confirming that they'd died of asthma and an overdose respectively. These days, anxious families would phone 111 or 999 – not a local GP who responds to them night and day. Not that the outcomes would have been any better........

Talking of nursing homes, in the 1990s it was still normal for a GP to help a patient in a great deal of pain or discomfort who had only a few weeks left that they were expected to live, to reach a comfortable death. This might be in a nursing home where an elderly resident with pneumonia had not benefited from a course of penicillin antibiotics and was progressively worse and 'not with it'. The GP doing the ward round of all ill residents in the home would suggest 'I don't think there's much point in prescribing Daisy another course of antibiotics, and it might make her nauseous. Does everyone agree?' He'd look round at the staff on the ward round, and they'd nod. If the family were there they'd be included in the decision. But that was it – the likelihood that extra treatment would help or extend her life was minimal. And everyone would then make her last few days more comfortable, mainly increasing her pain killers if Daisy was screaming or moaning in pain. Even in people's own homes, the GP would talk through the end of life possibilities with the patient and their family. They'd understand more about what the prescribed medication was for, and be able to increase the doses of pain killers or other comforting medication themselves.

But such trust can be abused when a doctor directs family members or care home staff to increase the doses of powerful painkillers, such as opioids, to help to manage someone's pain. The enquiry into deaths at the Gosport War Memorial hospital in Hampshire, England, found that 456 deaths in the 1990s followed 'inappropriate administration of opioid drugs' – shortening the lives of these elderly patients who thought that they were being safely looked after in that NHS hospital. This is another dreadful example of the abuse of doctors' power like that by Dr Harold Shipman, who murdered so many patients and got away with his cruel and selfish treatments for so many years. He was convicted of 15 murders but the Shipman Inquiry concluded that he had killed at least 250 patients, with his first being when he worked in Pontefract General Infirmary in 1971, and the last before he was arrested in 1998. The judicial review suggested that if only there'd been a brave whistleblower early on who'd shared their concerns, that could have saved and extended many people's lives!

Hospital consultants were there for the GPs too - with long distance phone support if you were called out to a very ill patient who did not want to be admitted to hospital but needed more specialised emergency care. I remember being called out to Ron, aged 73 years old in the late 1990s, to find that he was lying at home screaming with pain one evening. I examined his abdomen and it almost felt like he was pregnant. His bladder was super swollen because his prostate cancer was worse and blocking the urethra tube from his bladder, so all his urine had piled up over the last 24 hours and was trapped in there. I could see that there was not much point getting a catheter out of my car boot and inserting it up his penis as I'd usually have done as it would be unlikely to get through the blockage. I phoned a urology specialist at the local hospital – and in those days GPs and hospital consultants tended to be buddies, attending educational and other events together where they interacted. He directed me over the phone as to how to insert the catheter straight into Ron's bladder via an incision into his belly to bypass the cancer blockage. I'd never even seen such a procedure done before but I had a go and it worked – pints and pints of urine poured into the bag which I could then empty into a bucket. I thought Ron was at the end of his life but in this case 'no'. The hospital found ways to beat the prostate cancer and he could eventually pee normally and lived for another 15 years – in his own home and then with supported living, and finally nursing care.

And now?

Palliative care seems to be very well organised on the whole. It includes treatments to provide relief from pain and other distressing symptoms and integrates psychological and spiritual aspects of someone's care. The aim to is to put a series of support in place to help patients live as actively as possible until their death, taking into account their needs and preferences, and those of their families. But there can still be a problem about providing specific specialist care in a hospital ward of a different specialty. I was talking to a mental health nurse recently and she described how they have a severely demented patient on the end of life care pathway who has severe constipation. The other day there was no nurse on any of the mental health wards who had expertise in administering the enema that Dora needed inserting into her rectum. Barbara the nurse felt that she must read the instructions and just do it and it worked (so Dora's poo exploded from her anus!) – her mantra is that 'patient needs must come first'.

Dementia is more of a feature in a person's end of life these days. Dementia featured on the death certificates of nearly 90,000 people in England in 2023 for instance; and for about one in five of those registered as being on a palliative care pathway.

As people age, they often want to consider how they can have a *happy death*. That might mean moving out of the house they've been in for decades but are now living alone, and moving into residential care where they will be safer and less likely to fall. If they live at a distance from their families, and are at risk of falls as many older people are, then they need to plan for their older years whilst they are a bit younger and have full faculties. Moving into sheltered accommodation or residential care before there is an emergency health problem or crisis might well prevent the sudden deterioration in that older person's health.

Families need to consider the whole person in the end of life care that they talk through with their older, or ill, relative; and put the opinion of one doctor or nurse responsible for just one aspect of the person's medical conditions, into context.

But this inability to accept that we can let someone die peacefully is still rife. I recently heard from a hospital nurse about two care staff, Lynn and Emma, who had worked in a local nursing home for at least the last three years and still found it difficult to accept that a resident they'd become close to would soon die. One of their long-term residents Diana was admitted to a geriatric ward in the local hospital last week from a nursing home. She had many health problems and recently had had a major stroke which meant that she was bed bound. Even though there was a 'do not resuscitate' order in place and the family was happy with that and had agreed it, Lynn and Emma performed pretty aggressive cardio-pulmonary resuscitation (CPR) when they found Diana had collapsed, after one of the staff went into her bedroom to check on her at 7.30am. They both did CPR for about 30 mins from when they found her, to when the ambulance arrived. They couldn't just let her go without trying to revive her. By the time she was admitted to the hospital ward in a groggy state, she had four fractured ribs arising from all the chest wall thumping, and was in terrible pain trying to breathe. The hospital team admitted her and carried on doing all that they could for her, but she became more comatosed, and died later that morning.

The family were pretty angry about how the nursing home staff had resuscitated her despite the order not to do so being in place, so that Diana had a painful and confusing last few hours, instead of a peaceful death with family members being able to be by her side. Lynn and Emma had put their professional pride first in trying to provide the best CPR they could, instead of prioritising Diana's and her family's preferences for a comfortable death.

Specialist palliative care teams require people with specialist skills and experience such as: medical consultants and nurse specialists in palliative care, physiotherapists, occupational therapists, social workers, practitioners with experience in psychological or spiritual care, dietitians, speech and language therapists, pharmacists, specialists in interventional pain management – as well as GPs and their general practice teams. Wow!!! Quite an advance on the solo-care from the GP a few decades ago, who maybe called on a district nurse to help provide support for a patient living at home in their last few weeks.

Children and young people's palliative care focuses particularly on enhancing their quality of life and providing support for the family from when their condition is diagnosed. This includes managing their symptoms and the effects of their condition on them, anticipatory and parallel planning for what might be, and thinking ahead to death and bereavement. More children have life-limiting illnesses than most people realise. In England, the prevalence of children with life-limiting conditions rose from 32,975 children in 2001/2 to 86,625 in 2017/18; and these numbers are likely to continue to rise.

'Enhanced services' for palliative care for young people or older people are predominantly provided and funded by children's and adult's hospices and other charitable organisations. This includes services such as bereavement support, parent/carer support in the hospice or at home and much more. These services are still not routinely funded by NHS commissioners so hospices have to find ways to raise substantive funds themselves, so that they can keep going.

More than half of deaths in England currently occur in hospitals or hospices, but the proportion of people dying at home has been increasing for at least two decades. This trend is projected to continue, with deaths at home and in residential care homes expected to exceed the number of deaths in hospitals and hospices by the 2030s; even rising to three-quarters of all deaths by 2040. In my experience, and that of others, people do appreciate being helped to aid their loved one to die at home, especially if it is a child or young person where close family members can say a fond goodbye and stroke their hair or body, in their last hours. A new policy that has been brought in can allow an informal carer (a family member or friend) who has been trained, to administer medicines via an injection just under the person's skin to help with providing immediate symptom relief as part of palliative care, when this mode of treatment has been agreed with their clinician(s).

A recent analysis by the Nuffield Trust analysis shows that the number of people dying at home in England rose by a third during the pandemic, and in 2023 was about 28% of 544,000 deaths in England, with a further 20% of deaths being in care homes and 43% in hospital. About four-fifths of those who die in hospital attended A&E at least once, in their last month. And over 90% of people who died in care homes had at least one interaction with their general practice team in their last month of life. It is really important that people have access to the right care outside of hospital at their end of life, including that from their GP practice.

The analysis of those who died between June 2020 and February 2021 as the pandemic raged found that people who died at home in the most deprived areas received 2.2 interactions with their GP on average before the pandemic, compared to 2.7 interactions for people living in the most affluent areas. During the worst of the COVID pandemic this gap widened to 3.3 interactions in deprived areas compared to 4.2 in more affluent areas. On average too, people in the most deprived areas were prescribed 50% fewer medications to manage their pain and symptoms, compared to people in the most affluent areas. The proportion of people with at least one general practice interaction in the last month of life rose from 64% pre-pandemic to 75% during the pandemic and the number of interactions per person also increased. 38% of people who died at home during the pandemic were prescribed at least one medication to help them to manage their symptoms, compared to 34% before the pandemic. Another report relays that one in four people have three unplanned hospital admissions in their last year of life. So, these findings highlight the significant health needs of people approaching the end of life, as well as relaying evidence of unmet need, and inequalities in people's access to care, and the need for us to respect a person's choice for their options for a peaceful end of life.

Hopefully the creation of the NHS Integrated Care Boards in England and more integrated team working elsewhere in the UK, will engage staff from different health and care settings in underpinning patients' end of life pathways and support their earlier discharge home after treatment in hospital. They should be able to bring in new types of staff like social prescribers to help to provide palliative care, by aiding the psychological and social needs of patients in these link worker roles.

The shift to community based care should reduce the burden on hospitals, and make the most of the provision of virtual care, adapted to patients' and their families' needs and preferences.

A nearby hospice, the Douglas Macmillan hospice in North Staffordshire, that was founded in 1973 had 28 beds then. In the 1970s, local GPs provided medical care to the hospice, like they would do now for a care home. Now they employ around 450 staff, 235 of whom are clinicians, many working in community teams providing palliative care services across North Staffordshire. These teams work with a range of generalist health services such as GPs, pharmacists and district nurses. But the annual income needed now is at least £17 million per year, of which £3 million comes from the NHS, £5 million from their 21 charity shops, with many gifted donations as well. The hospice provides services in the community as well as maintaining inpatient beds, especially to help people to stay at home. If someone lives alone/wants to die at home, there is some staff capacity to stay with the patient for 24 hours a day in the last week of their life. Nowadays 40% of patients that the hospice provides care for have non-cancerous conditions causing their expected death, such as motor neurone disease, stroke or dementia. Decades ago, 90% of patients that the hospice cared for had cancerous causes of their end of life – so this reflects how people were exposed to harm in the industrial era and the higher proportion of people who died from lung cancer and mesothelioma then.

This conundrum over who should be funding hospices is widespread. Another nearby hospice in Stafford, Katharine House Hospice, continues to offer freely available specialist care to local people living with incurable illness and their families, for 1,500 families every year. The charity relies on the local community to help generate three-quarters of the funds that they need to run its palliative care support services, and their charity shops are a very significant part of their fundraising efforts too.

Assisted dying is often in the headlines these days. We hear in the news that every eight days or so a person from Britain travels to Dignitas in Switzerland for help to die. The absence of an assisted dying law in the UK forces people to take drastic measures to be in control of their death such as travelling abroad to end their life when they are weak and frail.

More than 350 Britons are said to have now ended their lives at Dignitas. That is not a comfortable end to someone's life to travel thousands of miles when they are in great pain and distress and usually alone too - for if family members go with their loved one(s) and are present during the ending of their life process, they face the risk of prosecution and possibly many years in prison when they return to the UK!

Public opinion in the UK has been in favour of assisted dying (also termed 'voluntary euthanasia') for many years. Though some of those in favour do not realise that this means 'providing people who have less than six months to live with lethal drugs to end their life', as opposed to 'giving people the right to stop life-prolonging treatment' which is a choice that any adult already has. Assisting someone to end their life in England, Wales and Northern Ireland is a criminal offence that could generate a prison sentence of up to 14 years.

The Netherlands was apparently the first country in the world to legalise euthanasia in 2002; they are extending the existing Euthanasia Act to even allow parents to opt to euthanise a terminally ill child younger than 12 years old, if all treatment options have been exhausted. Assisted dying was legalised in Canada in 2021 (termed 'Medical Assistance in Dying'), but fewer than one in 20 deaths end that way at present. There is interest among some MPs in our current parliament to launch a private members' bill for discussion on legalising voluntary euthanasia and physician-assisted suicide; and similarly to discuss a possible bill in the House of Lords. But, if doctors are involved in delivering assisted dying they have a major professional concern - how can they move from their role of preserving life, to one of accelerating its end?

I believe it should be a person's choice as to how and where they die, when they have been reliably told that they have a substantive life limiting condition. The problem is to enable a terminally ill person to make an informed choice, balancing their doctors' views (that might be influenced by their own personality - maybe a medical optimist and/or by their depth of knowledge - maybe as a specialist?) and their own preferences and beliefs, so that they can make the most of the limited time they have left to live in a dignified way.

A recent poll suggested that almost three-quarters of adults living in the UK support changing the law to allow doctor assisted suicide for people who are suffering from a terminal illness.

There are powerful arguments on both sides of this debate. Some doctors feel that their patients should have a choice about the timing and manner of their death, whereas others could make a conscientious objection and not get involved with individual patients.

Any changes to UK legislation to allow assisted dying would need to include multiple checks and balances in the pathways to preserve patient safety and enable the person to select their own informed choice of treatment. But the UK can learn from other countries that have legalised voluntary assisted dying.

Chapter 11. Digital transformation of healthcare – very trying!

I've actively pushed on the need for everyone to embrace various forms of technology enabled care across the NHS for the last 15 years or so. So much could be improved in the delivery of health and care services by using simple, readily available technology, to interact with patients and service users, and accelerate the potential for supporting people to improve their own health and wellbeing. Using one or many more digital routes via their phone or tablet is the norm for most people these days in their everyday lives - like Facebook, WhatsApp, video calls, text messaging, apps; and using wearable technology like smart watches for monitoring how far they've walked, or checking their pulse rate or setting themselves reminders. Personal digital assistants like Alexa can relay updates on the weather or signpost interesting information. All of these devices or functions could be used more widely than they are now to empower people to look after their own health and wellbeing. Digital delivery of care **can** cross traditional boundaries between hospitals and general practice, and between community teams, social care workers, mental health professionals, patient groups, informal carers... providing better, more coordinated services with clever IT so long as patients are engaged and have the right equipment, digital skills, know how and motivation. But does it really work out?

I supported a tech innovator Phil, in 2010, who had devised a telehealth interactive texting option to load onto a person's mobile phone, however basic their phone was. We got doctors and nurses to start using the service, combining familiar everyday technology (via the patient's mobile phone) with the psychology to engage individual patients in taking more responsibility for their own health and wellbeing. The clinicians could view the individual patient's responses on their computer screen in their surgery, and access biometric readings texted in by the patients as a graph, relaying progress such as weight loss or their blood pressure measurements. The initial pick list ranged from the shared clinical management of respiratory conditions like asthma, raised blood pressure, diabetes of all types, mental health problems, underpinned by promoting good lifestyle habits (e.g. by smoking cessation) and prevention.

Helping people with real time advice to minimise any deterioration of their health condition, so boosting their health and wellbeing, and avoiding future unnecessary hospital admissions. Within three years from the concept, the innovative service has been adopted by 26 NHS organisations throughout the UK; and clinicians had designed over 150 clinical protocols that were shared between subscribers to this Florence texting service. These protocols and connected resources provided intelligent algorithmic tools supporting clinical decision-making and informing patients about reliable self-care which they were motivated to adopt. Our UK government was interacting with the USA at an international level, sharing experiences of our early adoption of this telehealth service, which led to a nationally funded trip to Washington for our team in 2013, to share our insights about adopting telehealth at scale, and initiating the design of an Annie version of Florence telehealth for Americans to use. The Department of Health also invested £500,000 to underpin the roll out of this Flo telehealth asset across the UK then, for which I was responsible with the owner, Phil, who was officially recognised as the NHS Innovator of the Year, in 2012.

I was reading an interesting article recently that compared the use of telehealth (defined as telephone or video calls between patient and clinician) by doctors working in primary care (such as general practice settings) in ten different countries across the world, including the USA, Germany, Australia, New Zealand, Sweden as well as the UK. They found that these days, the majority of primary care doctors (who were sampled at random) found it easy to implement telehealth when providing patient care, and in the UK 82% described implementing telehealth as 'very' or 'somewhat' easy, which was the highest score in the ten countries surveyed; whereas only 30% of German physicians gave similar ratings. Drilling down, 72% of the 2000 or so GPs surveyed in the UK, thought that telehealth allowed them to assess an individual patient's mental or behavioural health needs remotely, to a 'great' or 'some' extent.

How it was

I'm not sure that I can recall when exactly it started to become the norm to use technology in my clinical role as a GP, or as an academic writing up research projects. Apparently, it was common in the 1800s for doctors to keep private medical notes describing the patient care they were providing. When the NHS was created in 1948, GPs were starting to keep a written record of individual patients on their Lloyd George mini-record card, and these were still the norm decades later. My memory of medical records in general practice in the 1970s, 1980s and 1990s, is writing up my patient consultations on these white paper cards with blue lines for a male and red lines for a female patient, on which we scribbled handwritten notes (in ink- not pencil!) and then stuffed them in the person's own bulging beige envelope pack. These record cards were even smaller than A5 size and were posted on to another general practice when the patient registered there after moving house.

There was some pressure for general practices to move to A4 size paper records in the 1960s and 1970s but primary care teams declined to do that. In the 1970s and 1980s there were trials of computerised medical records in general practices across the UK. Dr Preece, a GP based in Exeter is known to have been the first to use a computer in their consulting room, with a subsequent small pilot of an electronic records system funded by the Department of Health. This was when email was starting up too, via a programme that let users send messages across computer networks. In the early 1980s, less than 5% of GP practices were using computerised systems, but by 1992, 80% of practices were using electronic records and by 1996, 96% of general practices were doing so. Email interactions became much more frequent in the 1990s, slowly replacing the faxing of medical records and clinicians' letters by medical secretaries. The passing of the Data Protection Act in 1998 gave patients the legal right to access their own health records. But the NHS has a poor track record for creating a connected, national IT system that offers a single electronic health record that can be used by all health and care professionals. And there are still a small minority of Hospital Trusts that have not yet fully converted to using electronic patient records, and thus have mountains of paper-based folders still. A recent review of 182 Hospital, Community and Mental health Trusts in England, reported that 4% only used paper records, 25% were fully electronic and the remaining 71% of Trusts used a combination of paper notes and electronic patient records. The British Medical Association recently estimated that around 13.5 million working hours are lost each year in England of doctors' time thanks to the inadequate NHS IT equipment and lack of interoperability between the computer systems in different NHS sites. The out of date 'legacy' IT systems and hardware in so many NHS locations just do not seem to be up to the challenge of creating a sustainable, modern, digital healthcare service that links all the local health and social care providers in relation to the patient management that they share.

And how digital healthcare is taking shape now

The NHS 111 service has proved a popular way for people to be signposted to access the right care in the right place. There are more than 1.5 million calls a month at present. The most common advice to the caller is to contact their general practice, with about 12% advised to attend an urgent care centre or their local A&E.

Social media does have a role to play in interacting with, and updating, patients about their local health services and opportunities to improve their wellbeing. In 2016, I led on a project to create public Facebook pages for about 30 general practices in Northern Staffordshire for communicating at scale with their patients. The proportion of practices using Facebook shot up quickly in the next couple of years to about 90% when they saw the advantages of it. The practices' Facebook pages served as informative platforms, allowing the general practices taking part to share similar health promotion messages, for example aimed at promoting 'flu vaccinations or warning about high pollen levels; as well as aiding them to share updates with their patient population about their services. The messaging used by the North Midland's breast cancer screening team included animations to engage women and minimize their fears about how the screening was done. They targeted the practices in local Staffordshire areas where the mobile breast screening van service was due to be located for eligible cohorts of women, complementing their traditional means of advertising in local newspapers. This Facebook promotion resulted in the uptake of breast screening of women aged 50 to 70 years old shooting up by 13% in these local areas. Other social media routes such as Twitter (now X) and WhatsApp have helped to underpin other successful behavioural interventions too, such as helping to increase people's physical activity.

Digital exclusion
We have to remember that around 7% of households in the UK still do not have internet access in their home – especially those in some rural

communities; and around 13 million adults in the UK are estimated to lack basic digital skills too, to use tech devices such as smartphones (even if they can afford them!) for their healthcare. These elements of digital exclusion affect many people living in deprived communities who are more likely to be in poor health, due to their poor lifestyle habits and increased likelihood of having one or many long-term health conditions. Half of the 13 million people who are regarded as having low digital literacy are over 70 years old and more likely to need to access healthcare, and many others lacking digital skills have substantive mental health problems. Some other older people are just not interested, or get very frustrated, in going online to access healthcare services or their bank account, and distrust the IT systems, much preferring an in-person approach.

People need to be digitally literate to be able to access their medical records, as well as possessing a tech device. I was talking to Jo recently, who is a practice manager in a general practice in a deprived area. She is very aware of digital exclusion and how that applies to her registered patients. In her practice she estimates that 80% or so of patient consultations are face to face and 20% are online or by phone. Patients are given a choice of the mode of delivery of care, and encouraged to attend in person for urgent health reasons – as the doctor or nurse then thinks more widely about the whole person, considering possible health issues of which the patient had been unaware. Younger patients' choice of consultation is usually by phone. To reduce digital exclusion, the practice patient participation group (PPG) comes into the waiting room twice a week, to be available to help individual patients who are lacking confidence/competence to use their phone or iPad for a remote consultation by, for example, a video-call.

Tech challenges
The challenges regularly encountered by community nurses using tech as a norm in their daily working lives include short battery life, unsuitable hardware and software, old and cumbersome laptops, authentication challenges, use of multiple platforms, lack of integration between computer systems and combating the continuous repetition of doing data entries. Ergonomic issues feature frequently in nurses' feedback, with heavy laptops triggering back pain as the nurses sit working whilst in their

car writing up patient records, or accessing details about their forthcoming patient before their next home visit.

Healthcare provider organisations, commissioners and policy makers still need to undertake national, regional and local reviews of Wi-Fi internet connectivity in all geographical areas where their services are delivered, and understand how this is directly impacting on the work of clinicians, delivering care in people's homes and other community settings.

The rollout of existing and new health-tech equipment and services across the NHS and social care providers of a local population has historically been pretty slow because of poor coordination between organisations, a lack of resources so there is not a mass issue of the same equipment that inter-connects, and territory guarding. There is often a problem of interoperability between different IT systems that operate in hospitals, general practices (that use different computer systems run by competing national businesses), community and mental health settings, and social care. They often don't 'talk' to each other, even though various staff from different organisations are looking after the same patient and need joint access to the patient's medical record to be able to update it.

A patient may not need a smartphone or Wi-Fi in their daily lives, but they do need it for relaying biometric readings or conducting online interactions. On the one hand, enhancing digital delivery of care has the potential to help the NHS reach out to a wider group of people, increasing efficiency and lowering operational costs. On the other, digital exclusion for those without this access to smartphones or other devices or without the digital skills to operate them, is very worrying if it exacerbates health inequalities, especially for those who live in deprived populations where health problems are more common, resulting from their poor lifestyle habits and other pressures.

Virtual care
The COVID-19 pandemic sped up the adoption of virtual clinic consultations and remote patient monitoring, with many more patients and clinicians using various modes of digital technology in 2020 onwards. This helped people who could not travel and were stuck at home, elderly residents in care homes, and vulnerable patients such as those with

cancer who needed to isolate from others. Now, a few years later a large proportion of outpatient appointments between a hospital based consultant and patient are done remotely using digital technology, and patients are more able and willing to submit biometric readings, such as their blood pressure or oxygen saturation levels in their bloodstream, to their responsible clinicians who are based miles away.

This focus on virtual care across the NHS is unfortunately exacerbating digital exclusion for the general population, by benefiting more young, middle class patients who are well able to use digital technology and have the equipment to do so, compared to older or disadvantaged patients who cannot afford the tech devices or lack digital skills. Remote consulting can be more risky too for older people who might be hard of hearing, or who downplay their symptoms; or those whose first language is not English. I heard about Pauline the other day from her neighbour. She is 80 years old and has no internet access, no smartphone, and "She wouldn't recognise an app if it bit her on the bottom". She can't get a kidney function test done because her general practice has delegated this to a firm that deals with such blood tests via an app.

Some patients really do miss the patient/clinician, in-person communication through virtual contacts, and feel that they get less out of virtual consultations compared with face-to-face appointments. They are less likely to talk more widely about other personal matters when on a video call or telephone consultation, which then might turn out to be related to their clinical condition – so the right treatment might be delayed or missed. And signs might be invisible too without a physical examination when a patient is on a focused virtual interaction with their doctor or nurse, resulting in missed diagnoses and inadequate treatment.

An elderly patient may rely on their carer(s) and family members to relay clinical information about them to the remote doctor or nurse, which may give them a sense of insecurity about their subsequent virtual consultation. So, video-consulting does not seem to be used as frequently now as it was during the COVID-19 pandemic.

Some people do like online consultation – not just to save them time, but because they struggle to communicate with their clinician in a traditional face-to-face consultation, and male patients are more likely to report preferring this option.

Virtual group consultations enable groups of patients who have the same or similar health condition and challenges, such as the menopause or diabetes, to come together remotely with an adapted online version of face-to-face group consultations. This still enables the delivery of routine care including clinical input, lifestyle advice and reassurance. People can receive clinical and educational advice and guidance from their clinical facilitator, whilst also getting advice, input and support from other patients in the group - a great way to receive peer support from others in a similar situation to you. This promotes a better understanding of a person's condition, hearing how others are managing as they share experiences in a safe setting. A recent trial of a virtual group consultation for menopause treatment in London worked out really well. As many as 25 women with menopausal symptoms joined in most of the weekly sessions (18 were from ethnic minority backgrounds and/or lived in a deprived area - so there was a good mix of women taking part), led by local GPs. They were given access to further virtual group meetings with a dietitian or woman's health physiotherapist as required. Their menopause-specific quality of life scores improved by over 50% over four months - a great success.

As a GP friend Dr Jack said to me recently: 'remote care can make life easier for the practising clinician and some patients...but mustn't be used as a shortcut.' The use of remote consultation should complement and enhance normal NHS service delivery, not replace face-to-face consultation between a patient and their doctor or nurse. There have been many stutters in getting digital transformation underway across the NHS. That means that all health and care professionals, and their support teams need the digital skills that include the confidence, capability and capacity to deliver care via a range of digital modes that suit the needs and preferences of their patients, as well as themselves. Providing safe remote consultation is a complicated process. Staff need to understand what specific patient consent is needed, how to ensure that a patient is in a private room for the virtual consultation as they are too, which conditions or symptoms or signs are safe to be seen remotely, and what issues definitely or possibly (such as headaches, breathlessness, abdominal or chest pain) require a face-to-face assessment rather than a remote video consultation or phone call. And how can staff safely send photos of a patient's skin lesion say, to the secure email account of a distant hospital consultant, whilst minimising any potential medicolegal issues, if there is a risk of it being a skin cancer but the photograph is not very clear? The technology used for delivering healthcare and enabling self-care needs to be as intuitive and user friendly as possible.

I do prefer face to face appointments but I quite like it when my GP sends me texts...

Me too – first time I can read his writing in 25 years...

Many doctors and nurses choose a telephone option as their preferred remote type of consultation, as opposed to video-consultation for which they feel less competent and confident, and may find setting up and running the video call more demanding. This matches many patients' preferences too, especially if their access to technology that enables a video consultation, is limited. Adopting remote consultation can cost more than you might assume – a recent estimate of comparative costs of a range of different types of consultation between a GP and their patient, ranged from £14 for a GP face-to-face appointment in their general practice surgery, £9 for a GP telephone call, and as much as £38 if the GP triaged the e-consultation (taking around five minutes of their time) which then resulted in a further face-to-face or telephone consultation with a GP.

We've got to improve our NHS offer and sustain it as a public service – to everyone across the UK 'from cradle to grave' and not let the private sector exacerbate health inequalities as it is currently doing. Retaining our workforce is a vital element in that. For instance, many commercial companies have moved in, to take advantage of the interest in digital healthcare. Babylon Health became increasingly popular with customers signing up for the NHS *GP at Hand* app, so that by 2021 the company had more than 100,000 online-first patients on their list. Matt Hancock the then Health Secretary, was renowned for promoting *GP at Hand* from 2018. It had started up in 2014 as a telephone appointment service. Many general practices were up in arms as the company had enticed a high proportion of their younger adults who were in good health to sign up as NHS registered patients. This resulted in conventional local GPs being left with a higher proportion of their registered patient population being older, and so being more likely to have complex health conditions and limited access to technology for their personal use and healthcare purposes. And it was also difficult for *GP at Hand* patients when their health problem(s) meant that they should be seen in person, if the nearest clinic for a physical appointment was as far as 15 miles away. Babylon did extend its *GP at Hand* service to register NHS patients in Wolverhampton and Birmingham, so the conventional general practices were left with proportionately more older and sicker patients on their registers there too. Babylon pulled out of that arrangement several years later.

Going Online

All members of the NHS workforce who have a role that involves direct interaction with patients (so that's administrators and managers, as well as clinicians) need the digital skills to enable them to provide technology enabled care services more effectively. And many staff still do not have these skills. The types of technology enabled care they provide should meet users' needs and preferences, and there are many gaps there too. The main challenges concerning the adoption of technology for providing or accessing healthcare are patients' ownership of suitable devices such as a smartphone or tablet, and their digital skills too. And sometimes devices such as those for taking personal readings of a person's blood pressure or blood oxygen levels are loaned and then have to be given back – which can create disruption in their medical treatment if they cannot afford to buy their own device.

Many staff and patients still have concerns about how safe data storage is when linked with their medical records. There have been cyber security attacks on NHS IT systems and people are increasingly aware of this type of safety hazard.

Most patients can (if they have a smartphone or other device, and the digital skills) access their own general practice medical records, view their test results and book appointments via the online service that their general practice provides and promotes. Text messaging is a commonly used route in general practices that enables staff to invite large cohorts of patients to use the online booking link to make an appointment such as for a 'flu vaccination. The invited patients can then click on the booking link and verify their identity and choose a time slot from the sessions given as being available to them. This aids the general practice workflow, with much less time spent contacting patients individually, and that frees up the practices' phone lines too.

One example of an expanding online service, Patients Know Best (PKB), has been used in the NHS since 2008, with gradually more Trusts becoming interested in adopting it. It offers patient access to records of their historic hospital visits, test results and appointment letters, and interacts with most local general practices' online patient records too. So, this is a shared record including the latest up to date information about a patient's treatments, medications, allergies, and care plans. The patient can share this information with their pharmacist, family members, carers, or anyone else who is supporting them too. As of 2024, there are 4.2 million registered users in the UK (for whom it is free and accessible in the NHS App), with more than 20 million test results received on the platform each month.

The other side of the argument about making medical records fully accessible for patients to view, is the fear that many clinicians have about the possible repercussions that could result. These include the potential strain on general practice teams if patients viewing their notes want to discuss the content of a letter or their medical record with a doctor or nurse, to understand their condition(s) better, or drill down into a particular test result or health episode from many years ago. This might increase patient anxiety levels too, or incur unforeseen risks to patient safety. Some doctors fear that there may be increased litigation risks – especially if a patient is reading medical records from years ago when a doctor might have been more blunt as to how they described the patient, or wrote down acronyms like TATT (tired all the time) describing them unfavourably in their patient record.

Some new IT systems in general practice are seemingly not very patient friendly. For example, a local general practice that has been taken over by a Mental Health Trust has set up a booking system on a website and I've been told by Mike, a patient registered there, that a patient cannot book an appointment with a GP or other practice staff any other way (not by phone or face-to-face) without going via this access point on the website. This has led to quite a few patients switching to register at a neighbouring practice where the GP partners are personable and friendly and inclusive, and their patients can book appointments as usual by phone or in person, as well as online.

GP practices are independent, self-employed businesses and so have an individual approach to how digitally capable their staff are. Some do not have an online ethos and patients still cannot book appointments online even in 2024; Nick was telling me that he still has to phone in to his practice between 8am-10am and speak to the receptionist who then completes a request form for an appointment with a doctor or nurse, a blood test or a prescription; but then she can book Nick an online appointment with a doctor, or access online blood results to relay to him – this just doesn't make sense!

The NHS App is a great success story. Since this free app was launched in December 2018, more than 34 million people in England have signed up to it (as of June 2024) to get access to view their health records, order repeat prescriptions, nominate their preferred pharmacy, book GP appointments, register for organ donation, and/or manage their hospital appointments. There was a missed opportunity during 2021 when the NHS launched a separate app for people's COVID-19 passes, rather than simply adding them to the NHS app which would have led to a huge number of people installing it on their devices and using it long term. More new features are being continually added. The new digital transformation plan for the NHS includes overhauling the NHS App as one of the priority areas for development. It is seen as a 'front door' to NHS services, but this mainly applies to primary care, rather than hospital services. Although in the month of December 2023 in England for instance, 3.4 million secondary care hospital appointments were viewed by the patient via their NHS App, and more than 72 million prescriptions were ordered via the App that year. Another advantage is the money saved by sending information to patients via the NHS App for those who have opted for this form of notification, as opposed to a text message or letter – which was the norm until recently.

Virtual wards
Virtual wards provide an alternative to in-patient care in hospital (some call it 'hospital at home') – with a patient-facing app or website, a digital platform for the healthcare professional to access or utilise, and associated medical devices for taking the relevant biometric measurements. The doctors and nurses providing that remote type of care rely on digital technology and patient (or home carer on their behalf) recorded and relayed observations, about their clinical condition(s), so that they can make effective decisions about what is the most appropriate remote patient care to provide. Patients in a virtual ward can expect to be reviewed daily by the clinical team via a remote 'ward round', delivered by staff across integrated multidisciplinary teams. Patients can receive care in their own home or a nursing or care home, when allocated to a virtual ward. Just as for any remote consultation, care delivered in any virtual ward needs to be underpinned by robust clinical pathways, with clear inclusion and exclusion criteria applied to each patient, and an ongoing quick responsive service if any relayed biomarkers portray significant clinical deterioration of the patient. Virtual wards allow patients to remain at home in familiar surroundings, which can help to speed up their recovery, encourage their shared management with the overseeing clinician(s), whilst freeing up hospital beds for inpatients who need them most. So, the patient on the virtual

ward needs the equipment (bought by them or lent to them) to check their temperature, heart rate, oxygen saturation level, blood pressure and respiratory rate – that they can relay to the responsible remote clinician by wireless technology or text.

My first step getting involved with creating virtual wards, was in helping individual clinicians to use electronic stethoscopes. For example, a GP in their own surgery might interact with a nursing home manager who they can see by video link, who has person-to-person contact with one of their residents, in a private room. The nursing home staff member can then place the digital stethoscope, in relation to anatomical landmarks, on the front of the patient's chest or their back to capture their heart beats or breath sounds whilst the GP listens in real time, based miles away in their own general practice site, with that patient's medical records open for viewing on a parallel computer screen. Another option might be to record the patient's heart or lung sounds and send them directly to another clinician to get a second expert opinion if needed. I managed to get funding to buy 120 digital stethoscopes which cost around £170,000 in all with associated guides, and organise for a very intelligent junior doctor to provide 'how you do it' support to any recipient of the e-stethoscope who wanted help. The funds were from a pool of NHS money immediately available to set up COVID-19 care in April 2020, so the project was rushed through, leaving little time for training the doctors and nurses in primary care and nursing home staff as to how best to use their e-stethoscope – which all had to be done at that time via distance learning and remote support. We created a webinar to showcase how to set up and use the digital stethoscope. And also managed to include funding for four large nursing homes to set up a more advanced Tekihub kit that enabled care staff to relay biometric readings too, such as blood pressure and oxygen saturation levels to the remote doctor or nurse, alongside the live heart and breathing sounds of individual residents. BUT (there's always a 'BUT' with a rushed project) many of the GPs and senior nurses taking part were not able to overcome all the difficulties of setting up the system, getting it running, organising for their time for listening to match that of the nursing home staff who were placing their digital stethoscope where needed on selected patients etc. So many of the clinicians taking part backed out and didn't get the most benefit for their patients' care out of using their digital stethoscope for providing timely, informative, virtual care.

Another example I led on in providing long-distance virtual healthcare, was trying to detect if a person has an irregular heart rate (atrial fibrillation or AF) that needs sorting or treating when it is only happening every few days – but their clinicians suspect that they really do have AF, but that needs to be proven before blood thinning treatment can be started. Detecting AF can be challenging if it is paroxysmal like this, and was doubly challenging in the context of the COVID-19 pandemic when seeing patients face-to-face was so difficult. We found a way to address this in five Staffordshire general practices by issuing holters that selected patients could wear for up to 14 days, that analysed their heart rate and rhythm over that period and dispatched this patient record to their responsible GP, to act upon. We confirmed that a good number of people had AF in this way who could then be treated with a blood thinning medication and thus avoid the high risk of getting a nasty stroke in the coming years. Our team were recognised as national AF pioneers for this project, in 2022.

A consultant nephrologist (kidney specialist) recently wrote to the British Medical Journal relaying how well video consultations are going for patients who have had a renal transplant – and how the patients and their carers welcome the remote interaction with their responsible clinicians, rather than trundling up to frequent outpatient clinics.

But if the patient on a virtual ward should start to feel unwell and deteriorate, there must be systems in place during daytime and out of hours, to quickly alert a clinician who can initiate step-up care, reducing the likelihood of an emergency re-admission. Many virtual wards use reliable apps, wearables and other trustworthy medical devices enabling clinical staff to easily check in and monitor their patients' recovery status, record readings and enable them to make decisions about any changes in treatment, with local shared care medical records. A blended approach is possible too, with some remote monitoring as well as face-to-face care that best fits the clinical needs of the patient who's being looked after in a virtual ward, with a personalised care approach based on what matters to a patient that matches their individual strengths and needs. There should be shared decision-making between the patient and their responsible clinician, when deciding on the delivery plan for current and future treatment, with a personalised care approach.

It is expected that the establishment of virtual wards and linked clinical services can help to avoid up to a fifth of emergency hospital admissions through better support for vulnerable patients at home and in the community, to enable a patient's early discharge from hospital.

One study reviewing the use of virtual wards found that the average length of stay in a virtual ward was 7 days and only 14% stayed in their virtual ward for more than 10 days. Another recent trial of virtual wards in Leeds, saved an estimated 959 bed days in the first six months period in 2023 by providing an alternative to hospital admission, or their much earlier discharge home from hospital with follow-on virtual care.

The national urgent and emergency care recovery plan is to scale up virtual wards in England, to treat up to 50,000 people a month, aiming for 40-50 virtual beds per 100,000 population. At present in 2024, there are thought to be just over 12,000 'beds' available in virtual wards in England. Accelerating the extension of virtual ward beds will require more interactive working too between NHS and social care staff from different settings who share responsibility for the same individual patients, with monitoring hubs, and better continuity and alignment of staff, processes, clinical protocols and technology. These arrangements need individual patient and carer empowerment and support, and informed consent. Of course, you have to take these numbers and statistics with a bit of a pinch of salt – those patients registered as being based on a virtual ward may just have been popping into their GP surgery for regular checks for a short period – they wouldn't necessarily have been admitted and monitored in a hospital bed.

A local junior doctor recently described how the eight bedded frailty ward he works on in a hospital in Cheshire provides follow-up care for those who are discharged early to a virtual ward as well (with up to 50 patients at a time being managed virtually by remote clinicians). The frailty team have direct access to their patients' GP records via the general practice computer systems. They then have the power to stop or alter medications, or refer a specific patient to another clinical service. Some local practices are wary of the frailty team having this extent of access and control of their patients' records and treatment, and have refused to take part in the programme; but most local general practices have embraced this. Sometimes the overseeing frailty consultant will see a patient registered with the virtual ward in person, in the emergency department for follow-up, or in one of the outpatient clinics. The frailty consultants spend time reviewing patients on a virtual ward every afternoon, undertaking a comprehensive geriatric assessment which can take up to an hour.

Another good example is of an atrial fibrillation virtual ward where there were 50 admissions over an eight months period in 2022, when it was being trialled in Leicester. Twenty four of these patients were thought to have avoided in-person hospital admission with a further 25 readmissions avoided too - thanks to the remote monitoring and the patients relaying their biometric readings such as their blood pressure and oxygen saturation levels, to the overseeing clinicians based many miles away.

Surveys show that many members of the public are supportive of virtual wards and would be happy to monitor their own health and wellbeing in their own home, rather than being admitted to hospital, if that was viable and they felt safe at home. Collette (aged 66 years old) has recently been managed on a cardiac care virtual ward and was pleased with her experience "They have a virtual ward round like they do in hospital. I know that my readings are reviewed everyday by a cardiologist who is responsible for my care – just as if I was on an actual hospital ward. I trust what she tells me to do."

Artificial Intelligence (AI)
There's a wealth of opportunities for the NHS to embrace AI to improve the delivery of patient care and move to more personalised healthcare, by enabling machines to carry out health related tasks usually associated with human intelligence. For instance, using genetic results and analysing data on many similar people experiencing the same health condition(s) by machine learning, should help to select the most effective treatment for a particular patient. This might allow us to identify people at risk of a heart attack or developing a cancer at a much earlier stage, so improving their

chances of recovery. People's electronic medical records could be mined by AI to predict which patients have high risks of developing specific health conditions and offer them preventive interventions.

The ChatGPT product has had worldwide attention and interest recently. It uses a type of machine learning known as a *Large Language Model* which digests lots of text and data, and spots patterns to connect words within the text and from that, predict a logical sequence that addresses the initial challenge. But so far, what it comes out with isn't always logical or factual, and may have all sorts of glaring errors, so everyone in the NHS and patients need to be wary of the potential bias or errors that any 'medical' advice may contain. A recent study about its use by doctors involved three physicians scoring chatbot responses to 195 randomly chosen patient questions; chatbot responses were scored more highly than those from physicians in around four out of five cases. But there is still lots of discussion about the ethics and usage of AI such as ChatGPT, and concerns that students might cheat by plagiarising content for their own academic work. I've asked ChatGPT to review this book; look at the back cover and you'll see it's very complimentary!

So, the NHS workforce needs to understand the potential benefits and dangers of AI. Clinicians may distrust AI's functioning if they think that it exists for a commercial purpose, with insufficient input from patients or clinicians in its design, reliability and safety. But there's a great deal of hope that AI will continue to help in improving the early diagnosis of health conditions; and take over a substantial proportion of administrative work on the frontline, helping to solve the NHS workforce crisis. But any AI triage must be set up for the context it is used in - we still need clinicians directly involved who provide intelligent interpretation and analysis and take into account the whole person and do not just have a narrow IT focus on a person's reported symptoms.

Robots moving into health care?

Experts are talking about a new approach to managing type 1 diabetes with a step towards an 'artificial pancreas'. This recently released hybrid closed loop system, or insulin pump, could be life-changing for over 100,000 people in England with this type of diabetes if their condition is not well controlled, to reduce their risk of long-term complications from ongoing high sugar levels in their bloodstream such as blindness, amputation of a limb or foot, or kidney problems. Research trials have shown that this new technology could allow them to manage their blood sugar levels so much more easily and effectively with their insulin doses being adjusted automatically and monitored.

Recently, a woman described how her dream wedding was saved by surgeons who used a robot to remove her liver tumour, eight weeks before her wedding. And the operation went ahead as they promised – she recovered quickly and was able to walk down the aisle in her wedding dress, two months later.

A national 'smart hearts' project, has transformed the conventional heart failure pathway by using data from implantable devices which can then detect deterioration in any participating patient at an early stage and their treatment be modified so that their condition improves.

Robotic walking aids get national attention too in the media. A recent story was of Claire who suffered a serious horse-riding accident which meant that she was paralysed from the chest down. She's found the robotic suit to be amazing; her hands are free, and she can move around easily making the most of the parts of her body that aren't paralysed, by shifting her weight with the help of the suit.

An automated 'doctor's assistant' is being trialled that can phone up patients to discuss and assess their progress in recovery after surgery in hospital, to then free up the doctors who might otherwise have undertaken the calls, so that they can perform more complex care, that requires a real human surgeon. There are currently three ongoing trials of this application in London, Oxford and Hampshire hospitals for patients who have undergone cataract operations.

I DON'T FEEL I GET AS MUCH RESPECT NOW THAT THE ROBOT DOES ALL THE DIFFICULT STUFF.

In 2024 Royal Stoke University Hospital celebrated 10 years of providing robotic surgery. As a relatively early adopter of this technology in the UK, the numbers of operations have gone from 8 cases in 2014 utilising one robotic system, to over 600 procedures in 2023 using two of the very latest Da Vinci Xi systems. Although new competitors are arriving on the market each year these intuitive systems are still market leading.

Initially starting with robotic prostatectomy, consultant urology surgeons Mr Chris Luscombe and Mr Lyndon Gommersall performed the first procedure in 2014. Robotic surgery is now considered the gold standard for prostatectomy, with over 95% of these operations performed robotically across the UK these days. The length of time that a patient stays in hospital after such surgery is typically reduced by 70% compared with human hands-on surgery; a patient would usually spend just one night in hospital, and 90% of men are home after two nights – instead of a four day stay if they had had hands-on human surgery. Another key benefit from robotic surgery is the early return of a man's urinary continence, as well as their improved physical performance once they are home. If needed post- operative care after urology surgery can include patient self-catheter removal, supervised *virtually* by nursing colleagues.

Urology was the driving force initially for robotic procedures for Staffordshire, Shropshire and Mid Wales; gynaecology surgeons were close behind and now perform complex robotic operations too, utilising one of these two Da Vinci Xi systems. Recently a consultant gynaecologist at the Royal Stoke University Hospital (Mr Zeiad E-Gizawy) carried out five hysterectomies in one day, using the robot, with the help of fellow nurses, anaesthetists and other surgical staff; he reports that there are much lower complication rates with the robotic kit, compared with conventional laparoscopy procedures, and much quicker recovery times. Some specialist surgeons now perform complex colorectal surgery with robotics in the UK; and more recently collaborations between surgical specialties have developed multi-visceral resections with robotics, for example for complete pelvic exenteration – radical surgery that removes all body organs from a person's pelvic cavity. Overall Royal Stoke now has the broadest range of robotic surgical experience in the West Midlands and is currently debating the purchase of a third system. The adoption of robotics for more and more surgical applications is inevitable with cardiothoracic surgery and ENT (ear, nose and throat) surgery the next likely areas for extending and adopting robotic surgery, to replace conventional surgery practice.

The Royal Stoke University Hospital's urology team have showcased a range of robotic surgery on Channel 5's TV series' Critical Condition, highlighting the use of the technology and patients' positive perioperative stories, whilst undertaking a cystectomy (removal of the bladder) and partial nephrectomy (removal of a kidney part). The hospital is a leader too in robot assisted partial nephrectomy taking on more and more complex resections, whilst reducing patients' length of stay in hospital and improving patient recovery. Cystectomy outcomes have vastly improved with robotic surgery with a significant reduction in patients' length of stay in hospital from an average of 18 days with open surgery, to 7 days with robotic assisted radical cystectomy and ileal conduit diversion. Use of a high dependency unit for each operation has almost ceased and is only used for patients with other serious health conditions, so this helps to free up inpatient beds. Robotics has had exceptional educational value for the hospital staff too. To facilitate the day to day running of robotics, two surgical care practitioners have been trained to assist with the robotic workload. There are now many internally trained surgeons who have joined the Royal Stoke team as fellow consultants and have also been employed in a range of other hospital locations across the UK to spread their learning and experience of robotic surgery.

Virtual reality

Universities are increasingly using sophisticated simulated learning as opposed to conventional face to face teaching, that builds students' skills and confidence in participating in complex scenarios. Student nurses can do up to a quarter of their hands-on-training through virtual reality means. The Nursing and Midwifery Council has agreed that universities can deliver up to 600 of the 2,300 hours spent in clinical placement and classroom teaching via simulation training, as part of their three years nursing degree. The training can include wearing VR headsets with simulated actors playing patients of any age – from a baby to a frail elderly person.

Assistive technology

There is a wide array of daily living equipment and technology (also called assistive technology) available today that can help people to live more safely and independently in their own homes. So, these include any device or system that allows a person to perform a task that they would otherwise be unable to do, or increases the ease and safety with which they can perform such a task.

Smart devices allow someone to monitor and control their home settings from the palm of their hand, using a smartphone or tablet, or by talking to a smart speaker. Popular assistive tech items in the home include smart light bulbs, remote plug sockets, doorbells and security cameras. Smart speakers can help to keep someone connected with their friends and family too, so that they feel less isolated if living on their own.

Assistive technology might include substantial equipment like stair lifts, clever technology like exit sensors that can detect if a vulnerable person leaves their home, or aid their security, like a video doorbell. Or a simpler device like a daily pill dispenser can help older people to remember to take their medication. Self-monitoring of blood pressure with reliable technology, may give a truer estimate of a person's usual blood pressure than readings taken by a doctor in the surgery, allowing the remote exchange of a person's valid blood pressure readings, to help a clinician to make an intelligent analysis and maybe modify their treatment, saving time and travel costs for health and social care teams, patients and their families.

Using community alarms and other telecare technology can help people of any age and ability to live independently, safely and securely in their own homes. The assistive tech devices can be linked to a triage system where alerts can be relayed directly to social or health care teams, or family or friends. Such telecare services might be based on a combination of alarms, sensors (like motion sensors and door locks) with monitoring activities designed to raise a call for help if the pattern of someone's behaviour who lives there, changes. It can give family and friends peace of mind that they can be contacted in an emergency. A community alarm or care call system can connect the person at home to a 24-hour monitoring centre through a landline telephone link which can be activated by the service user pressing a button worn as a wristband or pendant. This then triggers an alarm call via a base unit to the monitoring centre and the trained and skilled operators can offer support or help to organise the care that they deduce the person needs. Any sensors or alerting devices are wirelessly connected and communicate with the centre via radio signals.

It is pretty obvious that sensible investment in assistive devices like motion sensors to detect when a person gets out of bed and switches on a light pays for itself, as the person is less likely to trip on their way to the bathroom, so avoiding costly in-depth care, that might otherwise have been needed if they had fallen and broken their hip. One project where I supported the GP inventor, Tom, was to trial his Bide prototype of motion sensors that work in the dark for instance when they get out of bed, to relay messages previously recorded from the frail person's friend or family member, whose voice they recognise – so that the frail person is more likely to cooperate with the relayed advice and take more care of themselves. It's difficult though for a beginner to get known at scale for their innovation, even if they can showcase the advantages in a pilot trial (such as preventing falls with this Bide device). These kind of aids tend to need international interest from a tech company to adopt it, produce it at an affordable cost and market it widely.

Smart plugs have a wide range of uses. When you're away travelling, you can use a smart plug to turn a lamp on at your home so it looks as if you're actually living there. You can start cooking your evening meal whilst you're at work, by switching your slow cooker on via your smart plug an hour or two before you expect to arrive home.

I led on a programme to try out how using personal digital assistants helped older people or others with health problems, during the COVID-19 pandemic. We chose the voice-activated device 'smart speaker', Alexa Echo Show as in 2020 it was the only affordable type that we could find with a screen. We had found that most of the vulnerable people we selected to help needed an Alexa device with a screen so that they could interact with a family member or friend at a distance, whom they could then see and not just talk to by phone. We managed to get funding for purchasing the Alexa devices (and sometimes associated SIM cards to enable internet connectivity at a person's home) and for students or helpers to travel to individual recipients' homes to help them to set up and use the device – from the local NHS technology enabled care budget and the local Council's Community Renewal Fund. Many of the 400 or so people to whom we gave Alexa Echo Shows were aged 50 to 90 years old; some had diabetes and others had a range of long-term health conditions such as multiple sclerosis, dementia, Parkinson's disease, depression and more. It was often difficult to get people's trust to join in and get a free Alexa Echo Show when they felt they were 'not worthy', not sufficiently tech able or were in a low mood – but we managed it. The devices had a real positive impact on the health and social well-being of nearly every user, and often their carers too. It enabled them to connect with a family member living miles away. Benefits they described were literally life changing for many of them – regular reminders for taking their medications or keeping appointments, improving their dietary choices, increasing their independence; and for those living alone, interacting with, and via, Alexa helped to combat their loneliness and low mood too.

One recipient of an Alex Echo Show was Alan, a 75-year-old male with dementia, type 2 diabetes, and low blood pressure which caused him to feel faint and dizzy. He lives at home with Ann, his wife. They used their Alexa Echo Show to: get twice daily medication reminders for Alan, set reminders for hospital and GP appointments (phone, in-person and now video-consultations too), speak to family and friends - local and miles away and for advice on healthy living – for example watch chair based exercises and try them out. The Alexa device reassured Alan, gave him confidence, and helped to improve his mental health and wellbeing. His daughter can drop-in on him virtually (to connect directly to his Alexa device, initiated from her end) to check that he is okay, and that her Mum is too. It's easier for Alan to communicate using an Alexa than by a traditional phone as he can see the person he's talking to. As well as providing support for Alan, this reassured his family, as they can see and hear that he is okay when he's alone, whilst his wife goes out to meet her friends or take the dog for a walk without the worry of leaving him on his own.

There are real benefits for the NHS too with the rising costs of managing e.g. diabetes accounting for 10% of the NHS budget, 80% of which is spent on treating the complications of poorly controlled diabetes. But we needed to be careful as some of the health advice and nutritional information relayed by Alexa to those participating in our project in 2021 originated from the USA and other sources; and specific diabetes information was not from a trusted UK organisation. So, for example the messages and guidance described a different type of blood test for people with diabetes that the NHS no longer used. We commissioned a local IT expert to add extra diabetes skills onto the Alexa service and members of the local diabetes patient group were very appreciative of having reminders that they chose, such as being prompted to examine the soles of their feet regularly to spot any infection or deterioration early on whilst it could be treated.

Using tech devices for self-care

Self-care is a continuum, as you take continuing responsibility for the daily choices you make about your lifestyle habits, such as (not) smoking or eating (un)healthy food. Self-care may also relate to your work/life balance, or hobbies - doing sensible physical activities rather than ridiculously extreme body building for instance. People can adopt various digital therapies to help them with their wellbeing. For instance, there is a vast range of informative online learning on many trustworthy websites, such as those run by national charities.

These days, so many digital aids can boost your wellbeing, whatever health conditions you might have. That could be via trustworthy apps, video-consultation with a clinician, social media channels such as WhatsApp or Facebook, telehealth or texting, online learning resources on recommended websites, digital access to your medical records; hopefully preventing deterioration of your health condition, wellbeing and/or improving your lifestyle habits. Digital cognitive behaviour therapy (CBT) for instance, lends itself to virtual learning, done by the user in their own home or another quiet space. They can learn to self-treat their depression or anxiety disorders such as post-traumatic stress and body dysmorphia via CBT techniques, with support from NHS Talking Therapies where a practitioner or therapist provides support, including regular monitoring and oversight of the patient's safety and progress.

If that's successful in improving their mental health it could mean that they can stop taking antidepressants prescribed by their GP, or no longer need mental health support – saving the NHS money, and improving the likelihood that the person stays in work if they've a job, or returns to work if they've been off work for a while, maintaining good relationships with family, friends and work colleagues.

The personal fitness app market has flourished over recent years, allowing the user to capture their past trends in related biometric measures, as well as their current performance. Setting doable targets can really motivate someone to sustain positive behaviour and good lifestyle habits, like increasing their daily exercise activities. Smart watches tend to have additional functionality too, with extra features such as calendars, messages and email notifications. Most require pairing with a smartphone to be fully functional, which makes them more expensive.

The Apple Watch can detect whether a person's irregular pulse rate is likely to be due to atrial fibrillation (though such a diagnosis would still need to be confirmed by their doctor or nurse). There are substantive risks with wearable technology too though, as well as benefits. Some tech devices (e.g. those without a CE mark) may generate data that is unreliable, or some self-monitoring devices may induce extreme competitive urges which are not healthy – such as losing too much weight. So, people should be aware of the limitations of every piece of technology that they use and not become overly reliant on it.

The World Health Organisation has been pushing its strategic vision for digital health to be 'supportive of equitable and universal access to quality health services' for many years. It sees digital health as a conduit to 'help make health systems more efficient and sustainable, enabling them to deliver good quality, affordable and equitable care.'

Community diagnostic centres

These centres are based in community locations such as shopping centres or health centres, and provide tests that previously were only available in acute hospital settings. They are popular with those invited to use them who have been called in for a scheduled test or scan. A local mobile endoscopy unit has just opened up near to me; the hospital overseeing the centre hopes (and expects) that by operating in a community site for seven days a week they can clear the waiting list backlog, and provide the diagnostic tests much more quickly in future.

And now?

The British Medical Association (BMA) is campaigning for a nationalised NHS IT service to be accessible by primary and secondary care, mental health and community care and other health and care organisations. Every health and care professional involved in a particular patient's care should be able to draw information out, or add information in to the same shared care record in a secure, straightforward way. So many clinicians, social care workers, managers and support staff need ongoing upskilling in digital delivery of care to enable digital transformation to really happen on the ground, focussed on proactive and preventative patient-facing care, as well as the delivery of reactive acute care.

There needs to be good cyber security in place to protect the privacy of patients' data in keeping with best practice relating to information governance. The national plan is to embed security so that if a breach does occur, healthcare organisations can respond effectively at speed with a reliable recovery plan. But there are still reports of very basic security breaches.

For instance, when the CQC did an inspection of a local practice's premises recently they found a board in one of the consulting rooms with lots of post it notes on it. When the inspector asked the GP who worked from that room to explain what these notes meant he confessed that they were his very many passwords – so anyone coming into that room, such as a cleaner, could have taken advantage and got access to patients' medical records pretending to be 'Dr John'!

And the large scale of the cyber security risks that abound in the NHS were really highlighted when several major hospitals were affected by a cyber attack in summer 2024. The hackers reportedly targeted software used by a private laboratory that provides blood testing services for the NHS. They demanded a ransom (which was not paid) and released highly sensitive data online that included NHS staff and patients' personal details – like their names, date of birth, and blood test results that had been undertaken in hospital and GP surgeries around London. As a result, thousands of surgical procedures and outpatient appointments had to be postponed, with some life-changing consequences.

There are potential huge dividends for the NHS if they invest in supporting patients to use the NHS App so that they can access their medical record, order repeat prescriptions online or book an appointment. Nearly 80% of the adult population in England has registered for the NHS App, but less than 20% use it monthly. BUT there will need to be substantive investment in that training and finding solutions for patients who cannot afford IT devices or lack the skills or motivation to utilise the NHS App – in local libraries maybe (if they are open!).

Chapter 12. Prescription for Change: 77 ways to save and sustain the NHS

Our NHS is suffering from underfunding, and is forever trying to recover from repetitive, disruptive reorganisations of the whole system and focused parts – mainly generated by political interference and their limited knowledge and intelligence about addressing patients' needs and preferences in patient-centred, acceptable ways.

The elements of our NHS that need to be improved and extended are its efficiency, effectiveness and accessibility, if it is to function well over the next few decades at least, and deliver top quality, accessible health and care services, that remains 'free at the point of use' for all UK citizens. Mind you the strapline 'free at the point of use' is commonly used by politicians and NHS top management as they brag about the NHS, to mask many of the failings that exist across health and care. We do need to remove politicians from their overall control of the design and provision of NHS and social care, work out what is affordable, then push on prevention and empowering people to self-care for themselves, if the NHS and social care are to survive. We need to plan for the future forecasts when we will have a larger, older and thus sicker population - with the number of over-65 year olds expected to grow by more than 20% in the next ten years.

We need to recognise and address the health inequalities that abound across the UK, that generate millions of premature deaths each year from unhealthy lifestyles, as well as so many health conditions like diabetes, or heart disease, or dementia that create miserable last years for so many older people. There are such inequalities in life expectancy and healthy life expectancy at birth, comparing those who live in the most, and least, deprived areas in the UK.

So, it's all about the **whole** picture – not just about repairing the **'holes'**.

So, please NHS bosses (whoever you are?) can you action all of these 77 ways to save and sustain the NHS in the next year or so? No more neglect, plasters or crutches for our NHS provision of healthcare.

We want the NHS to provide a comprehensive service across the UK, which is free of charge, based on people's clinical needs, and universally available to everyone. Switch these dreams, hopes, desires for the future of the NHS to achievable targets, and kick start the intensive care and underpinning workforce needed for the NHS to survive, as matters of urgency – **PLEASE!**

77 brilliant ways to save and sustain the NHS

Preserve and expand our NHS workforce:
1. Employ and train the number of staff we need for the delivery of NHS care; trained to make the most of their roles (e.g. all pharmacists able to prescribe medication) and meet patient demand.
2. Proactively optimise the health and wellbeing of all the workforce.
3. Ensure that staff have the right skills/capabilities/confidence for: the site and specialty where they work, the purpose of their role(s), levels of responsibility.
4. Encourage dual training/ qualifications for clinicians e.g. mental health alongside adult nursing; public health with other medical specialties.
5. Respect everyone's role – a porter may be as useful/as important as a hospital consultant! And create the same expectations of their training and quality of performance if their employment is outsourced by the NHS.
6. Retain NHS and social care staff – respect their quality of life, value their input across their NHS and social care career paths and their dedication to their roles.
7. Overcome blockers to increasing training numbers proactively, like the limited opportunities that there currently are for trainee placements in the community and hospitals – maybe establish and roll out simulated learning as a norm?
8. Value all primary care providers: dentists, optometrists, pharmacists, dietitians, podiatrists, as well as general practitioners – and their teams.
9. Improve staff retention by writing off student loans generated from university degrees for doctors, nurses, midwives, pharmacists, dentists and other health professionals, if they stay

working for the NHS for a minimum time e.g. at least half-time working for ten years.
10. Legislate for safe staffing levels and seniority across all NHS and care organisations; flag unsafe levels of workload – in all NHS and care settings; and take action in response to any issue, to minimise the chance of it happening again.
11. Recognise that international doctors and nurses in training need to feel valued by guaranteeing them permanent residence in the UK upon qualifying in their specialty; and thereafter.
12. Enhance the team culture for all staff, where their motivation to provide the best care that they can in their role is valued and linked with others in their team; which should contribute to their retention in the NHS.
13. Invest in new roles if the advantages are proven, such as social prescribers, physician assistants (or associates) and nursing associates, who currently provide a range of frontline interactions between general practice teams and their patients; but being clear that these are unregistered staff who do not deputise for nurses and doctors, and thus sustain the quality and safety of healthcare provision.

Reserve sufficient national funding for the NHS to be freely available for all, meeting all these 77 goals - soon and forever:
14. Agree fair public finances – enough for the sensible delivery of healthcare in all areas and types of care – the fair distribution recognising enhanced needs in deprived areas.
15. Set equal pay for staff doing the same job – whatever their gender/ethnicity or NHS employing organisation; unless the location justifies a different pay rate such as delivery of healthcare in a remote base, or expensive location such as a city like London.
16. Fund hospices with guaranteed ongoing NHS funds for everyday care, and reduce their reliance on charitable donations for providing basic care.
17. Upgrade NHS computer systems so that they are integrated across all health and social care service user facing services - so that all staff can share and access elements of the same patient records.

18. Fund the NHS through public taxation - recognise that older people, who are the majority of users, have paid their share into the NHS when they were at work as their 'passport to future care'.
19. Cut bureaucracy for general practices, and rebalance their income to focus on providing consistently good quality everyday patient care, rather than nationally imposed illogical targets.
20. Support the existence of traditional, local general practices and reverse the trends to closures and mergers by allocating a fairer share of the NHS budget to primary care; and consider purchasing GPs' premises to include in the publicly owned NHS estate.
21. Reinstate financial support for NHS care provided by all primary care specialists to enable access for everyone and shift care closer to home – to NHS dental care, optometry eye care, podiatry foot care, basic pharmacy provision rather than trendy special offers like urine testing (currently only available for the younger age group who are least likely to need the tests).
22. Evaluate the delivery of all NHS services at scale to underpin further investment decisions; but undertake this internally and fairly, and not via a highly paid external company with politically defined priorities.

Create an inclusive culture – for staff and patients:

23. Ensure that there is no sexism, no racism across the NHS (for staff and patients).
24. Treat people with disabilities fairly and equally.
25. Enable everyone in the NHS to treat their patients (and carers) with kindness, sensitivity, courtesy and respectfully; to support them to make informed decisions about their forthcoming treatment and care, whatever their ethnicity, gender or age.
26. Value coproduction - embedding a culture of engagement with service users (especially those with lived experiences) to design and improve the delivery of NHS services.

Uphold consistently high quality standards of delivery of healthcare:

27. Achieve consistent quality across the NHS – for all aspects of services, and all NHS organisations – no excuses!

28. Ensure prison healthcare matches prisoners' needs and characteristics; and is as good as NHS provision outside prison.
29. Set reasonable, achievable targets for the delivery and nature of care, that are as important to patients, as managers and clinicians.
30. Provide additional funding for early quality improvement programmes that include feedback and reporting on: outcomes, unintended consequences, and estimated benefits such as time and cost savings.
31. Balance the benefits of continuity of care with unproven short-term gains such as fast access to a clinician - even someone who is unfamiliar with the patient.

Prioritise prevention; enabling and empowering people to self-care:
32. Boost patient-centred care – listen to individuals, and groups of patients and the public at all levels, at all times; and act upon their suggestions and feedback.
33. Invest in the NHS and government departments in improving the health of the population – so that we have a 'health care service' and not a 'disease care system', which will in turn enhance our economic prosperity and help to keep people in work for longer.
34. Encourage people to take more responsibility for their own health and wellbeing.
35. Incentivise individual members of the public to improve their lifestyle habits and thus their health and wellbeing e.g. via free access to gym or sports centre or positive activities.

Redress health inequalities and improve population health:
36. Extend numbers of general practices in deprived areas/ with more staff of all levels and specialisms.
37. Ensure good access and facilities for all e.g. people who are disabled (with equipment to enable them to be independent), and those with poor English language skills.
38. National leaders must devolve responsibility to a community-focused system that prioritises primary and community care and reflects local needs and circumstances that include: rural settings, deprived populations, those with serious mental ill-health, varied ethnicity and different age groups.

39. Provide consistent access to screening for a range of health conditions, taking this to community sites as well as health and care settings (and extend some screening such as blood pressure checks to pharmacies and dental surgeries), where screening is likely to be taken up.
40. Enable vulnerable people to make personal decisions about their future healthcare by informed consent e.g. if they are nearing the end of their life and prefer not to have further investigations or treatment.

Integrate the delivery of health and care – so that everyone respects and cooperates with this multi-organisational working:

41. Focus on integrating mental health and social care, with hospital and primary care services, as well as the voluntary sector.
42. Underpin recognition and management of long-term conditions and comorbidities; mental and physical health - across all clinical specialties in hospital.
43. Provide follow-on care: patients must be informed and know what to expect and how their care will involve interactions between primary/community/secondary/ mental health care and social care.
44. Accelerate safe discharge from hospital to the right location with after-care that suits the patient's needs and preferences.

Provide and sustain great leadership – for all aspects of the NHS – from the top to team leaders:

45. Inspiration is essential from leaders – look for it, value it, and then inspire the younger generation of NHS workers.
46. Encourage leaders to stay in touch with all elements of the delivery of healthcare that are under their remit – valuing service users' and staff feedback.

Equip NHS managers to be able to do a great job:

47. Promote and appoint people to NHS management roles based on merit and experience – not on who they know/nepotism.
48. Reform how the NHS and other public services are managed, with the main focus being attainment of clinical outcomes, rather than political targets.

Ensure wide ranging availability of NHS services:
49. Make clear in language/routes that everyone can understand what services are available, and how to access them.
50. Agree attainment of current national targets that will demonstrate the improvement of our NHS in two (or even one!) years time e.g. the number of people waiting on a trolley for an in-patient bed for more than four hours (1%?) or the number of people waiting longer than 18 weeks on the elective care waiting list (none??).

Operate NHS Trusts and primary care providers as learning organisations:
51. Reflect, reflect, reflect: learn from everyone's feedback and experiences (such as patient reported outcome measures) – from leaders/ managers/ staff/ patients/ carers.
52. Create a continuous learning culture that generates actions in response to any harms that arise to minimise the chance of their recurrence e.g. incorrect medication or treatment, unsafe staffing levels.
53. Generate energy for change – not sloth.
54. Value complaints – from staff, patients, carers, and other health and care organisations; take them seriously and listen to the content and nature of each complaint.
55. Encourage anyone (staff, patients, service users) who has concerns about the delivery of NHS care or management to express their views and get the right people listening – so they won't think they'll be classed as a 'whistleblower', but rather a responsible member of staff or citizen. Consider if their concerns match the NHS's expected quality standards, and then act accordingly.

Maintain safety standards:
56. Set standards based on evidence and national expectations; and promote them at scale across all NHS organisations – and stick to them.
57. Ensure safe standards for patient care from all perspectives – for vulnerable patients, or their use of equipment, or people's possessions.

58. Encourage everyone to report concerns in a professional way with some evidence that can generate actions.
59. Set up systems in health and care to stop and spot fraud; create an alert system for confidential reporting; avoid, prevent the issue happening again, and take rapid action if it is suspected or proven.

Modernise the delivery of healthcare as far as is acceptable and affordable:

60. Invest in NHS infrastructure as well as the delivery of healthcare. Improve and modernise the structure and maintenance of community, general practice and hospital premises. Design and provide digital and IT systems across health and care Trusts and primary care providers, so that every NHS organisation is seamlessly connected to a single patient record. This includes investment in the delivery of remote care such as video consultations between patients with a clinician or carer, in any health and care setting so that technology assisted remote care management is available whenever, and wherever, appropriate to the service user's needs and preferences.
61. Enhance digital inclusion, so that those with limited access to tech devices or who have limited skills to use them, are not left out of receiving NHS and social care that suits their needs and preferences. Offer alternative pathways for people who cannot, or prefer not to, access tech and digital routes to the provision of health and social care.
62. Promote the NHS App to book appointments, view medical records including test results and referral letters, order prescriptions, contact clinicians and other staff; utilise public libraries and other community sites to help people to access online health services such as the NHS App.
63. Create the national framework for the adoption of Artificial Intelligence (AI) across the NHS to include the regulations, governance, guidelines and monitoring that are essential for embedding AI in the safe and effective delivery of our future healthcare; with ongoing feedback to improve the adoption and delivery through a continuous learning system.

Work with private healthcare providers in as far as it benefits the NHS:
64. Welcome use of private medicine by self-funding individuals, if that keeps NHS costs down and there are no unexpected consequences. Support patient choice in accessing a range of treatments such as alternative therapies or complementary medicines where there is some evidence of their effectiveness, or at least no risks from side-effects.
65. Help to balance the public/private ratio of funded care provided by dentists, pharmacists, optometrists, podiatrists, counsellors so that their services are accessible and affordable for the general population.

Welcome and evolve strong links between health and care providers, local government and the voluntary sector:
66. Appreciate volunteers – in care/health services; train and use them to utilise their talents and experience.
67. Go for an all inclusive, equal culture, system-wide so that delivery of social services is regarded as being as important as the provision of hospital care.
68. Appoint lay members on NHS boards to be independent, with enough relevant experience to scrutinise and relay their honest opinions in intelligent ways.
69. Value the voluntary sector, but check that they are dependable and fit with NHS values – invest in shared care as justified on track record and merit, not a political decision to award funds.

Minimise unjustified government interference:
70. Set NHS long-term goals/ funding that have been agreed by knowledgeable experts based on the structure, capacity, capability and processes needed to be in place to achieve affordable clinical outcomes – for all. Renew government policies to reflect these targets/ prioritise enough funding/ and do not prioritise 'quick wins' over long-term gains.
71. Overcome the current lack of accountability across the delivery of the NHS at local and regional levels.
72. Sustain change over the long-term; so, this requires a cross - governmental approach and cross-sector strategy which focuses

on wider health, care and wellbeing outcomes - rather than box ticking exercises.
73. Initiate cross-governmental action to tackle and redress people's adverse lifestyle habits for all age groups, that lead to obesity, lung disease such as asthma or lung cancer, heart disease, and other cancers such as liver and pancreatic cancer.

Celebrate the achievements of the NHS:
74. Enhance the UK profile for creating innovative health improving developments (like robotic surgery) and published research.
75. Fast track new, proven treatments – generated in the UK or abroad; re-establish and create joint research programmes across countries e.g. including academics working in Europe/other continents with the UK.
76. Learn from comparing lower (or higher) attainment for healthcare outcomes in the UK compared to other countries – What?, Why?, When?, How?
77. Make the most of NHS birthday milestones – exploit such timings to generate staff and patient and public support and appreciation of our NHS, and thus enhance its 'healthy life expectancy'.

Abbreviations

AA	Anaesthesia Associates
ABPI	Association of the British Pharmaceutical Industry
ADHD	Attention Deficit Hyperactivity Disorder
A&E	Accident and Emergency
AF	Atrial Fibrillation
AI	Artificial Intelligence
ARRS	Additional Roles Reimbursement Scheme
ASHA	A support organisation for asylum seekers and refugees in Staffordshire
BMA	British Medical Association
BMI	Body Mass Index – a measure calculated from the height and weight of a person
CBT	Cognitive Behavioural Therapy
CCG	Clinical Commissioning Group
CIC	Community Interest Company
COPD	Chronic Obstructive Pulmonary Disease
CPR	Cardiopulmonary Resuscitation
CQC	Care Quality Commission
DVLA	Driver and Vehicle Licensing Agency
ECT	Electroconvulsive therapy
ENT	Ear, Nose and Throat
EU	European Union
GMC	General Medical Council
GP	General Practitioner
ICS	Integrated Care Systems
IT	Information Technology – the use of computers

MS Teams	A programme by Microsoft to provide virtual meetings
NHS	National Health Service
PA	Physician Associates
PPG	Patient Participation Group
PKB	Patients Know Best
QR code	Quick Response code – a barcode that stores information in a pattern of squares
SHA	Strategic Health Authority
VR	Virtual Reality – a computer-simulated reality which people can interact with

Printed in Great Britain
by Amazon